WINNING CHECKERS

for Kids of All Ages

R.W. Pike

Illustrated by Scott Nelson

C&M Publishing Co.
24 Kris Allen Drive
Holden, MA 01520-1001
(508) 829-7752

ISBN 0-9635300-0-3

Printed by
Maverick Publications, Inc.
P. O. Box 5007
Bend, Oregon 97708

TABLE OF CONTENTS

TABLE OF ILLUSTRATIONS

TABLE OF DRAWINGS

FOREWORD

After an extensive search for a primer on Checkers for Children revealed nothing that I felt would be a helpful ally in enhancing my grandson's enthusiastic initial interest in learning and advancing his understanding of this not so simplistic lifetime board game, I undertook this writing.

The fascination of chess, which has long been looked upon as the most intellectually stimulating and challenging of board games, is well represented in numerous treatises for youngsters. But its difficulty for the beginner, child or adult, seems to make checkers an ideal precursor for anyone who wants to start chess.

With no desire for debate and only a hope to encourage the further pursuit of those who are interested in checkers and chess, I cite the following quote in the "Murders in the Rue Morgue."

> I will therefore take occasion to assert that the higher powers of the reflective intellect are more decidedly and more usefully tasked by the unostentatious game of Draughts [Checkers] than by all the elaborate frivolity of Chess. In the latter, where the pieces have different and bizarre motions, with various and variable values, what is only complex is mistaken (a not unusual error) for what is profound.

Edgar Allen Poe

I thank all of my family, friends, and my illustrator, Scott Nelson, whose unflagging support and good humor has been instrumental in the writing of this book. Special thanks to, and in memoriam of, Marium J. Pentland.

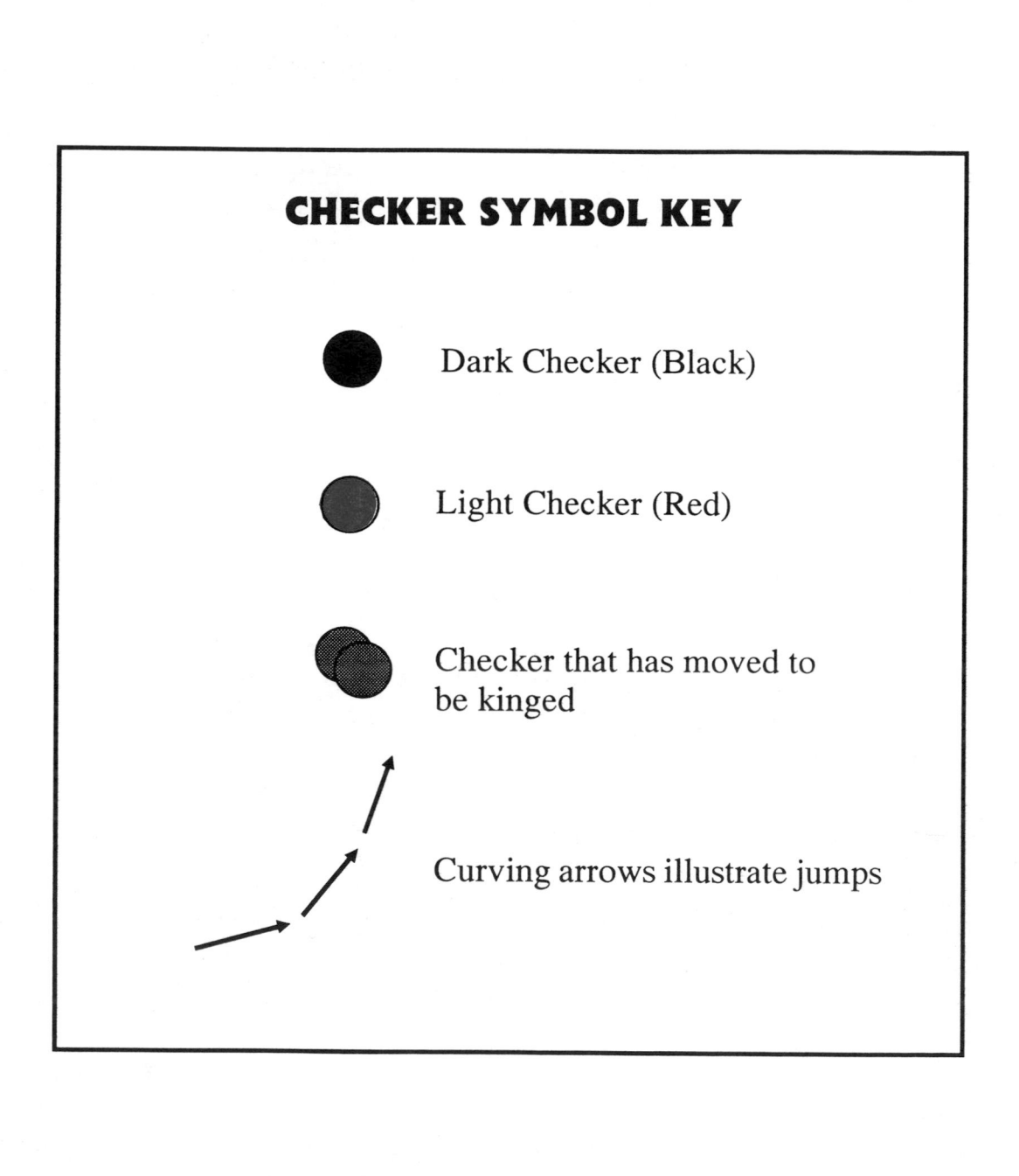

CHECKER SYMBOL KEY

Dark Checker (Black)

Light Checker (Red)

Checker that has moved to
be kinged

Curving arrows illustrate jumps

INTRODUCTION TO CHECKERS

Checkers is the oldest and most popular board game in the world. Nobody really knows when or where checkers started. The first time a checkers game was noted in history was with pictures engraved on King Tut's Tomb, of two players playing a game of checkers in Ancient Egypt over 3000 years ago!

Checkers is played almost everywhere in the world. It is played and enjoyed by people of all ages, from very young to very old. It is a game that you will be able to play and enjoy forever.

By learning to play checkers now, you will have a lifetime of fun with your family and your friends. Checkers is exciting to play. It is easy to learn. It has lots of surprises and awesome moves.

Checkers is a very fair game. There is no luck in checkers, only skill. The player who plays with the most skill in each game will win. Two players who play with equal skill will draw or tie, neither wins or loses. (Illustration 1)

To make it easier to learn, please use a checkerboard and checker pieces to set up the positions and practice each of the moves. Try doing this with the first two pictures. If you don't have a checkerboard and checkers, cut out the board on page 53 and follow the instructions that are listed with it.

In checkers, both players should enjoy themselves, win, lose or tie (draw). Remember that, when you play checkers, so you will have more fun and learn more every time you play; win, lose, or draw.

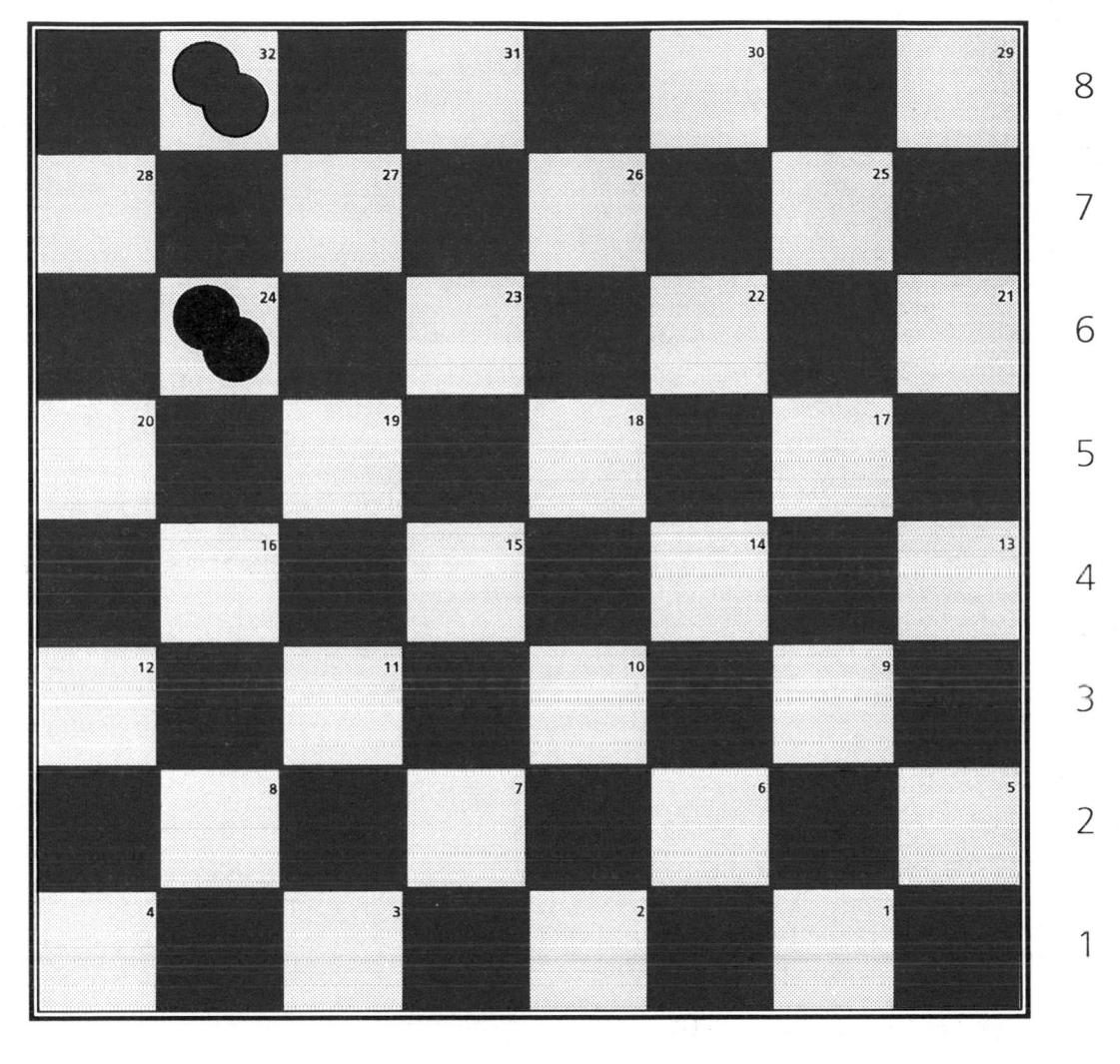

LIGHT SIDE

ROW

8
7
6
5
4
3
2
1

DARK SIDE

ILLUSTRATION 1: Light to move. It is a tie or draw because both Dark and Light have kings. Light's king is in a double corner so it can move to square #28 without being jumped and then Dark's king has to move away to square #20, #27, or #19. Neither player can force the other into a position where they can be jumped so the game is a draw or tie. NO ONE WINS OR LOSES.

LIGHT SIDE   ROW

8

7

6

5

4

3

2

1

DARK SIDE

ILLUSTRATION 2: Light to move, Dark wins because it is Light's turn to play and it has to move onto a square (#26 or #27) where it will be jumped and captured by the Dark checker on #23. That eliminates the last Light checker, leaving only the Dark checker on the board. DARK WINS!

OBJECTIVE OF CHECKERS (or Winning)

The objective of checkers, as in most games, is to win. You win a checkers game by capturing (jumping over) all of your opponent's pieces before your opponent captures (jumps over) all of yours. The winner is the player who has pieces still left on the checkerboard when all of the opponent's pieces have been captured. Look at Illustration 2 above.

4

THE CHECKERBOARD

The checkerboard is like a playing field. It is a large square board with 64 small squares (Illustration 3). There are 32 light colored squares and 32 dark squares. Checkers are played *only* on the dark colored squares. The light squares are never used. Look at Illustration 3 again.

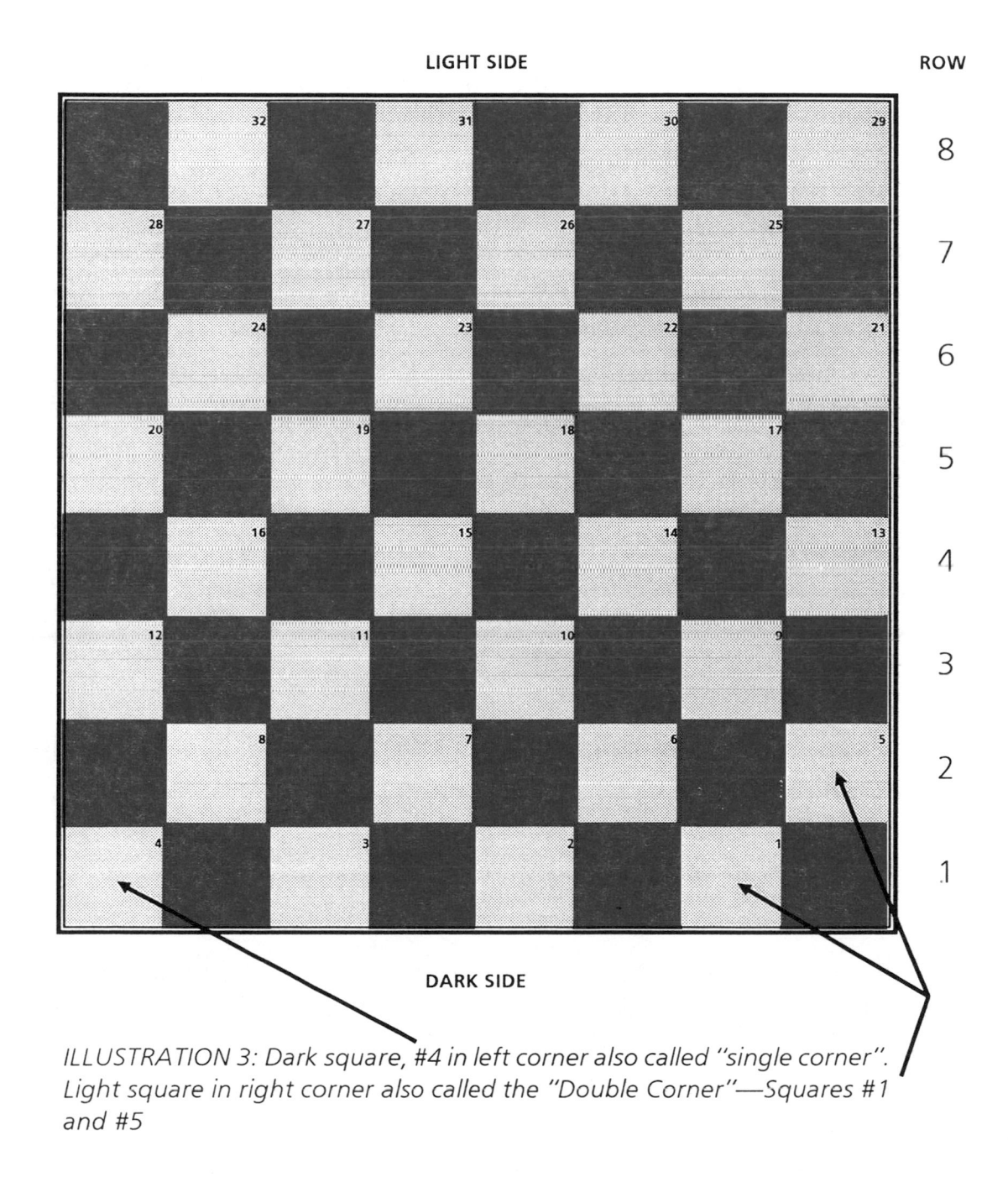

ILLUSTRATION 3: Dark square, #4 in left corner also called "single corner". Light square in right corner also called the "Double Corner"—Squares #1 and #5

WHERE THE CHECKERS GO TO START THE GAME

The checkerboard is always set up so that the left hand or "single" corner, is a dark square and the right hand corner is a light square. The dark squares there (#s 1 & 5) are called the double corner. (Illustration 3)

The 32 dark squares on the checkerboard are numbered one (1) through thirty-two (32) as shown in all the pictures. The numbers and rows make the moves easy to understand. You can use the numbers and rows to follow moves in this and other checker books.

There are also eight (8) rows of dark and light squares numbered 1, 2, 3, 4, 5, 6, 7 and 8 starting with number 1 as the first row nearest the dark end of the board and ending with row 8 at the far side or the row nearest the light end (Illustration 4).

The 12 Dark checkers go on the first three rows of dark squares on the checkerboard. These squares are numbered 1, 2, 3, 4 in the first row, 5, 6, 7, 8 in the second row and 9, 10, 11 and 12 in the third row. (Illustration 4)

The 12 Light checkers go on the last three rows of the checkerboard. These squares are numbered 21, 22, 23, 24 in the sixth row, 25, 26, 27 & 28 in the seventh row and 29, 30, 31 & 32 in the eighth row. (Illustration 4)

When all 24 of the checkers (12 Light and 12 Dark) have been properly placed on the checkerboard, it looks like Illustration 4.

DARK SIDE

ILLUSTRATION 4: Starting position with 12 Dark checkers on squares 1-12 and 12 Light checkers on squares 21-32. Dark moves one of the checkers in row 3 (#9, 10, 11, or 12) to row 4 (squares #13, 14, 15, or 16) to start the game.

Below is an example of a notated series of alternating moves by Dark and Light at the start of a game. Try making all these moves. Has anyone made a jump?

	Dark	Light
1.	10-15	23-18
2.	12-16	26-23
3.	8-12	30-26
4.	16-20	21-17
5.	9-13	17-14
6.	6-9	23-19

No, not yet.

CHECKER PIECES AND HOW THEY MOVE

There are only two kinds of checker pieces. Single checker pieces, which are called

checkers, look like this: 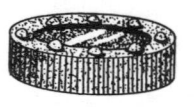 Dark  Light. Crowned, or

double checker pieces are called kings, kings look like this:

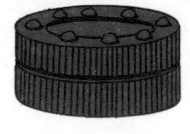 Light King  Dark King (Illustration 5)

8

Single checker pieces (checkers) are the only pieces that either player has at the start of the game. These single checker pieces or checkers can only move diagonally forward to an empty dark square in the row ahead. (Illustration 6)

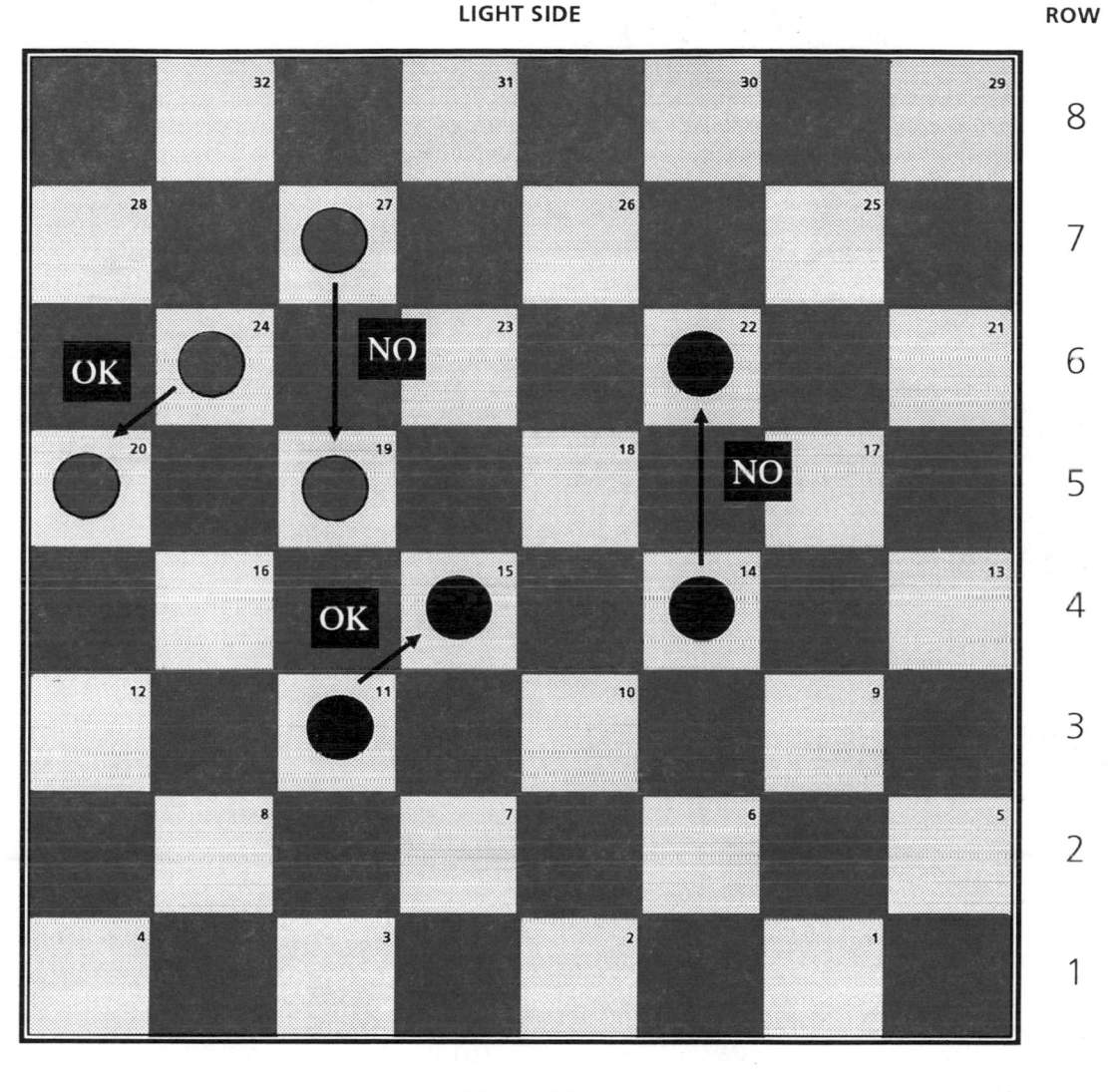

ILLUSTRATION 6: Checkers can only be moved on the dark squares. These are the squares numbered 1-32. The light squares are never used. You are not allowed to move from one dark square across a light square to another dark square. You can only move diagonally from one dark square to another dark square in the row ahead, if it is empty.

Or they **must** jump over and capture an opponent's piece, that is on one of the two dark squares diagonally in front of them if there is an empty dark square on the other side. (Illustration 7) This is hard to understand at first, but very important—so please look at Illustrations 6 and 7 again carefully and practice the moves on your checkerboard. Study Illustration 8 to learn more about the moves.

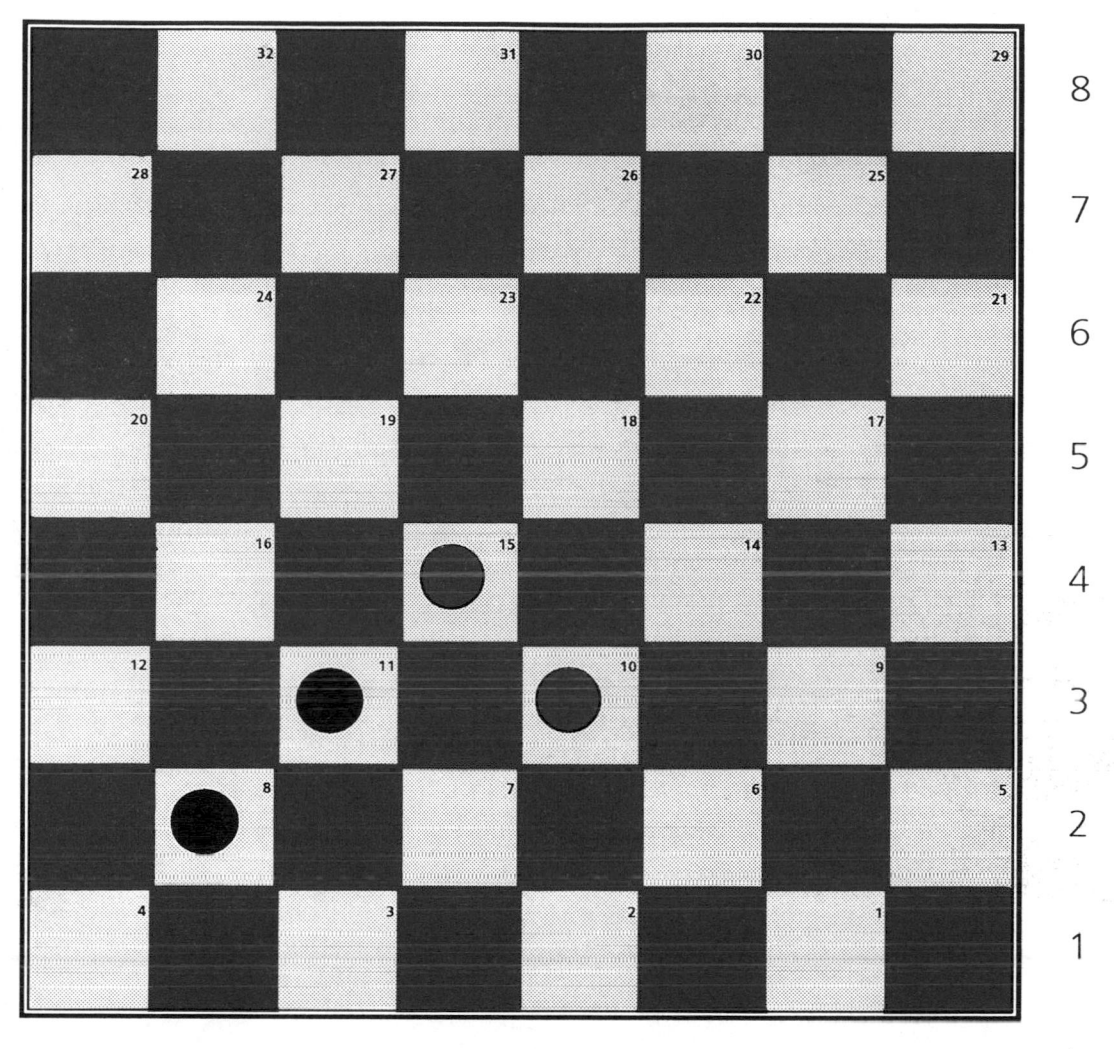

LIGHT SIDE

ROW

DARK SIDE

ILLUSTRATION 7: It is Dark's turn to go. Dark must jump over the Light Checker on square #15 because square #18 is empty. Dark cannot make any other move with either of the two Dark checkers. Dark must jump over the Light checker on #15 and stop on #18. When Dark does this the Light Checker is considered captured by the Dark checker that has jumped over it. The checker that has been captured is removed from the board. Whichever player captures all of their opponent's pieces is the winner.

8

7

6

5

4

3

2

1

DARK SIDE

ILLUSTRATION 8: The Dark checker on #11 can move diagonally forward to #15. It cannot go to square #16 because there is another Dark checker on that square. The Dark checker on #16 can move diagonally forward to #20, or #19 because both are empty. The Dark checker on #14 cannot move because both of the squares diagonally in front (in row 5) are occupied. The Dark checker on #18 is blocked by the Light checkers on #22 and #23 in the 6th row, but the Dark checker on square 17 can move diagonally forward to square #21 in the 6th row which is empty.

What moves can any of the Light checkers make? You can turn the page upside down to help you see the possibilities. Be sure to use your checkerboard to practice these moves so you understand

Answers—(A) #22 double jumps from #22 to #15 to #8 or single jumps #22 to #13. (B) #23 can move to #19 but would be jumped by Dark's #16. (C) #27 can move to #24. (D) #26 cannot move. (E) #25 can move to #21. (F) #29 cannot move.

These are such important moves that we are going to go over it again in another way to make sure that you know how the moves work. If an opponent's piece is in one of the dark squares in the row ahead of you on either side of your checker and there is an empty square on the other side of the opponent's piece, **you must jump** over your opponent's piece, to the empty square on the other side. (Illustration 9)

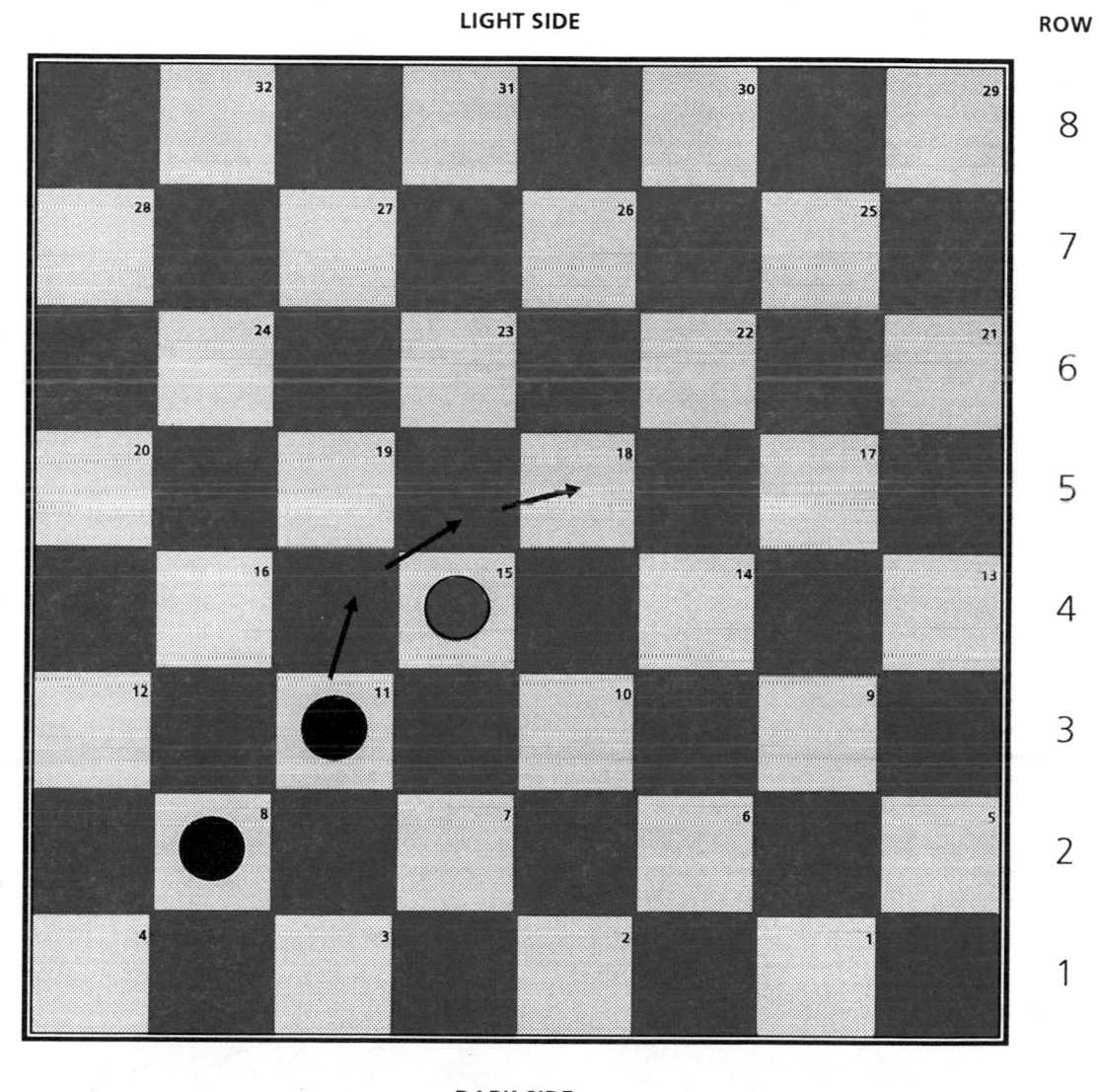

ILLUSTRATION 9: Dark's turn to move. Dark has to jump over and capture the Light checker on #15 with his checker #11, because #18 is empty. As soon as Dark jumps over Light he has captured it so he takes it off the board and puts it in his holding area.

13

When you do this, you capture your opponent's piece. As soon as you do this, you take the piece or pieces that you jumped over off the checkerboard (Illustration 9). The captured piece or pieces should be set off to the side.

Sometimes your opponent may make a move that will give you a choice of jumping in two or more ways with two or more of your checkers or kings (Illustration 10). When that happens you can take whichever jump you prefer.

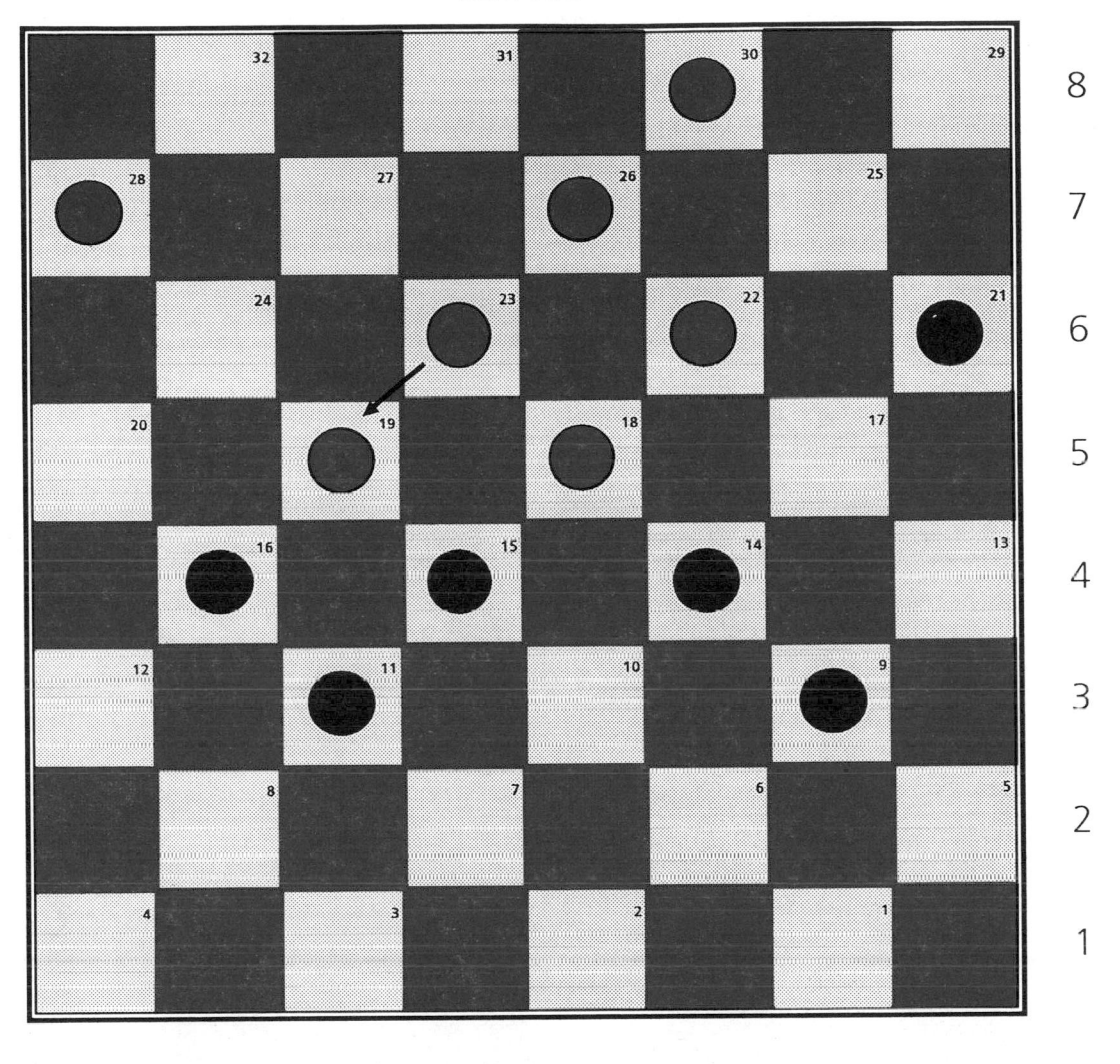

DARK SIDE

ILLUSTRATION 10: Light's turn. If Light moves from 23 to 19 as shown above, then Dark has three jumping possibilities. Do you see them? Dark can jump from 16 to 23, or from 15 to 24, or from 14 to 23. Which jump would be the best for Dark to take? 14 to 23 is best because it results in an even trade. Light will jump from 19 to 12, or from 19 to 10. But if Dark jumped from 16 to 23, or from 15 to 24, then Light would get a double jump back. Try it and see!

Sometimes you will have an opportunity to make a double jump and capture two of your opponent's pieces. You can make a double jump if there is an empty square on the other side of the opponent's piece in the row ahead and then another opponent's piece in the next row with still another empty square in the row after that! (Illustration 11)

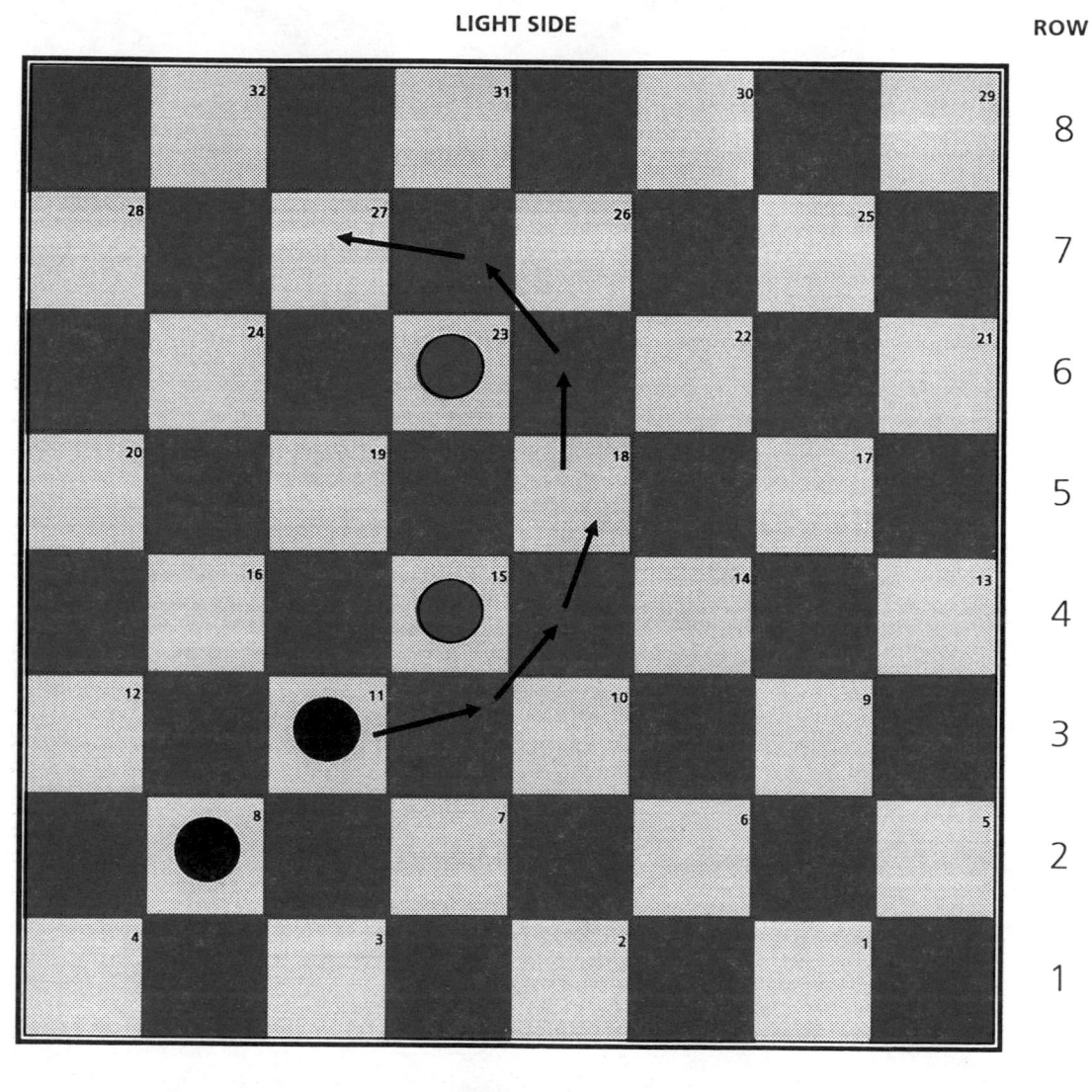

ILLUSTRATION 11: Here is an example of a Dark side double jump. Dark jumps two Light checkers on the same move capturing both of them and taking them off the board. Since there is no checker on #18, Dark must jump over Light #15 to square #18. Since there is no checker on #27, Dark must jump over the Light checker on #23 to #27. As the Dark checker jumps over the Light checkers, they are captured and taken off the board.

Once in a while, but not very often, you can make a triple jump, capturing three of your opponent's pieces in the same series of jumps. You can do this if there is still another one of the opponent's pieces left to jump with an empty space behind it in the next row after you have made a double jump. (Illustration 12) Another example of a triple jump is shown in Illustration 13. This is a very exciting move that often wins the game.

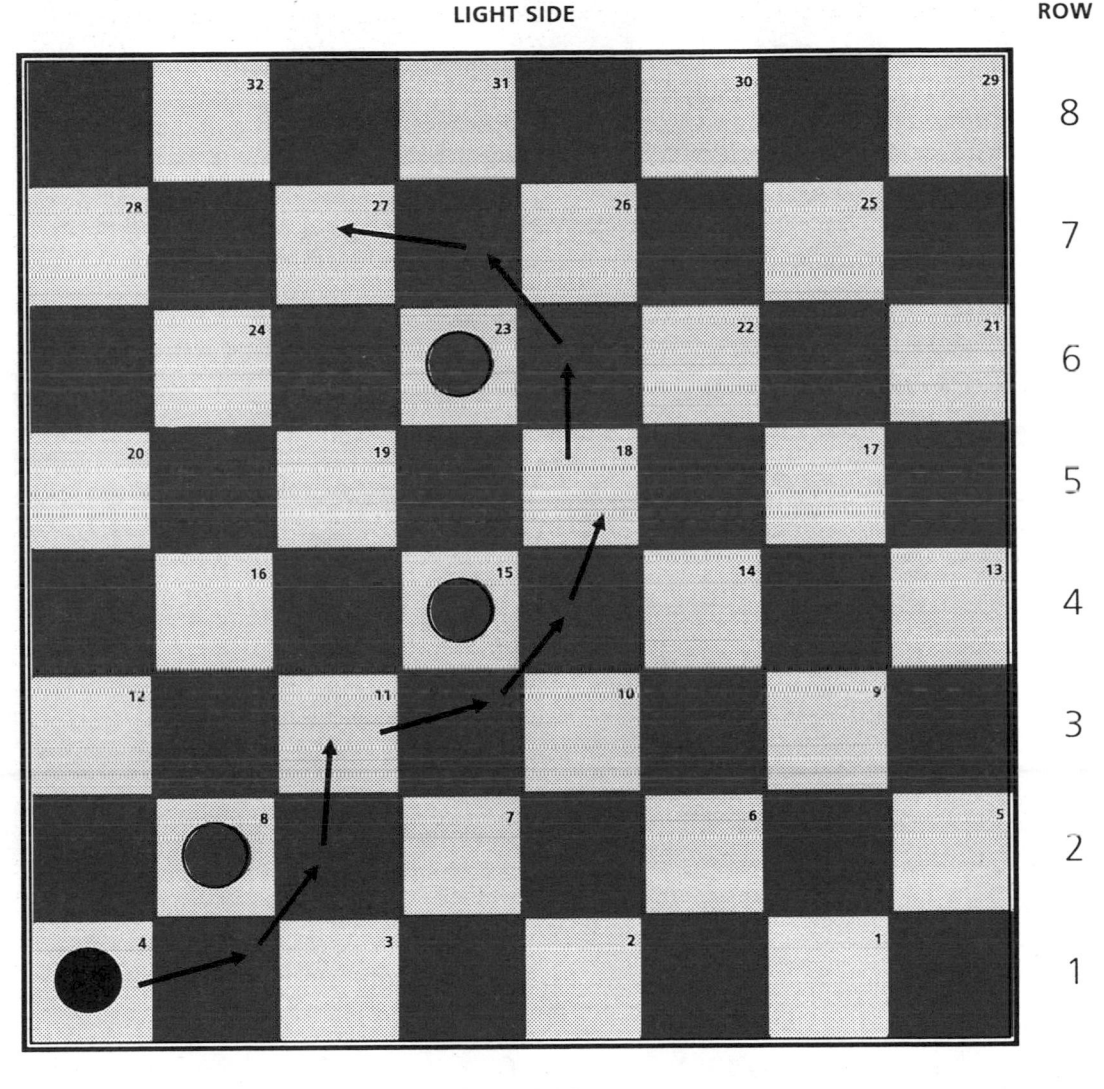

ILLUSTRATION 12: From this position the Dark checker on #4 has a triple jump and captures the Light checker #8 by jumping to #11. From #11 Dark jumps over Light #15 and captures it, landing on empty square #18. From #18 the Dark checker jumps over Light #23 and stops on empty #27, capturing the Light checker on #23. When the triple jump is completed Dark has captured all three Light checkers that were jumped so Dark takes them off the board.

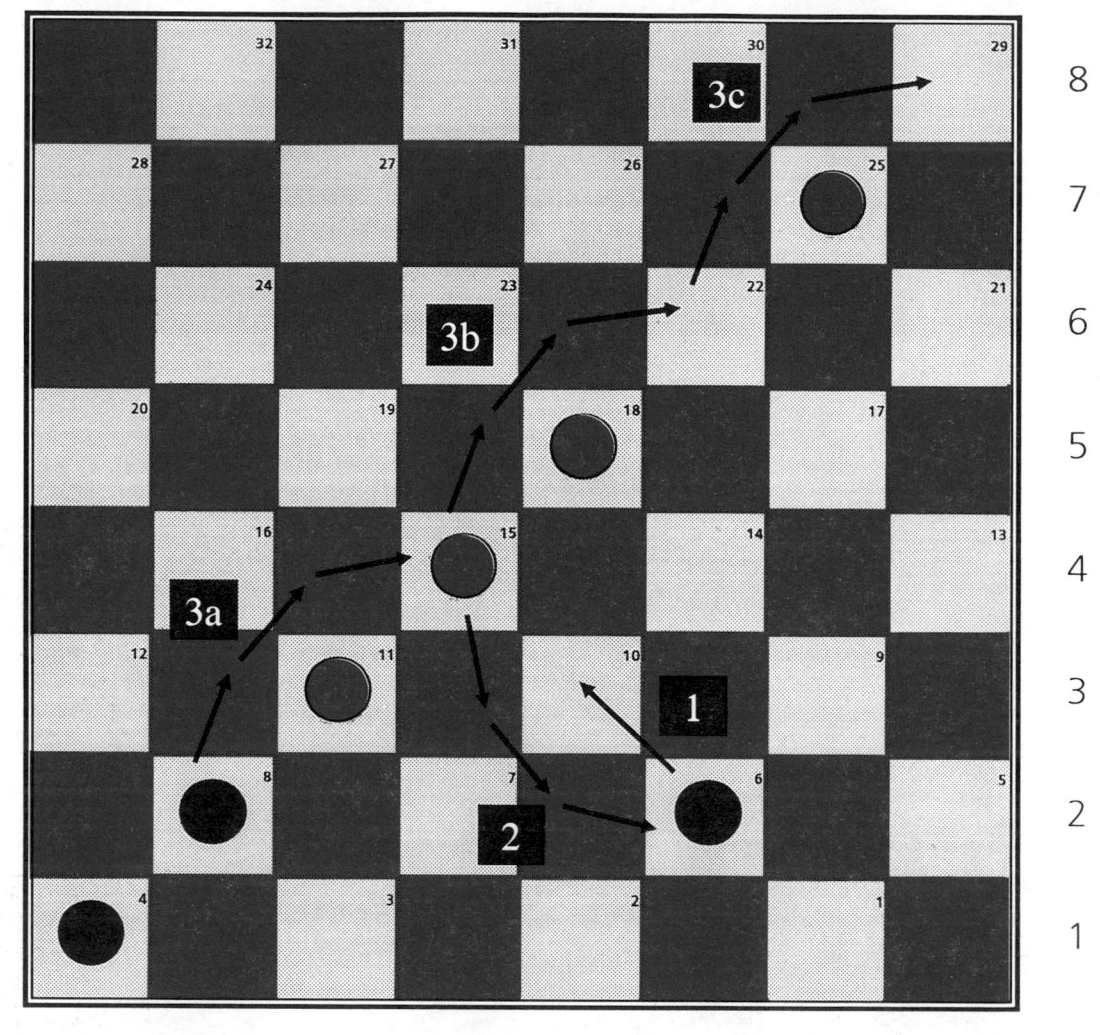

DARK SIDE

ILLUSTRATION 13: Another example of a triple jump for Dark. It's Dark's turn. Dark moves the piece on #6 to #10. A sacrifice move. Now Light #15 must move and capture Dark on #10 by jumping over Dark onto square #6. Then Dark has a triple jump going from square #8 to #15 to #22 and on to #29. (A great move and Dark gets a King!) Dark takes the three Light checkers that have been jumped off the board. Dark has almost won the game with this move because Light has only one checker left and Dark has two which is usually enough to win the game.

GETTING KINGS

Any single checker piece that moves by single square advances and/or jumps all the way into the last row on the far side of the board has reached the "King Row." (Illustration 14)

When one of your checkers, or your opponent's checkers, gets all the way to the "King" row (row 8 for Dark and row 1 for Light) it must stop there and be crowned or kinged. A checker that has reached the King Row must stop and be crowned a king. It cannot move again until the other player has taken his next turn.

Answers: *The Light checker on square 6 can get to the king row and be kinged by moving to square 1 or square 2.*
The Light checker on square 11 can get to the king row by jumping over the Dark checker on square 8 to square 4. That way it captures the Light checker and gets a king!

Illustration 14: In this picture the Dark checker that moves from square 28 to square 32, is crowned or kinged with another checker placed on top of it as shown on page 8. The Dark checker on square 21 that jumped over the Light checker on square 25 capturing it and landing on square 30 must stop and be crowned or kinged. It cannot continue on in the same turn or move and jump over the Light checker on square 26. Where and how do the Light checkers go to become kings? See answers below.

DARK SIDE

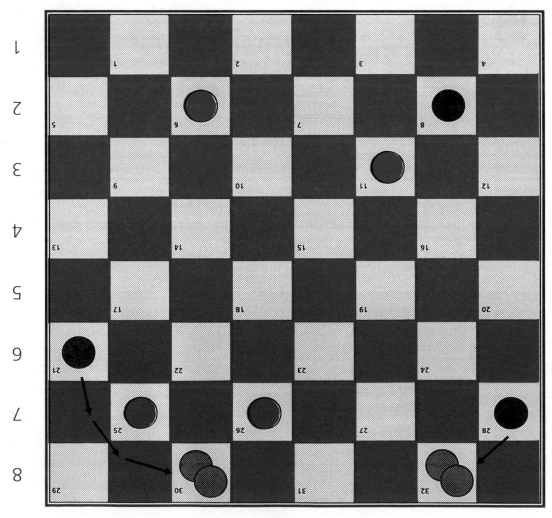

LIGHT SIDE

ROW

WHY ARE KINGS SO IMPORTANT?

Kings are very powerful double checker pieces. They are very powerful because they can **move and jump** diagonally in any direction; forward and/or backward, when it is their turn.

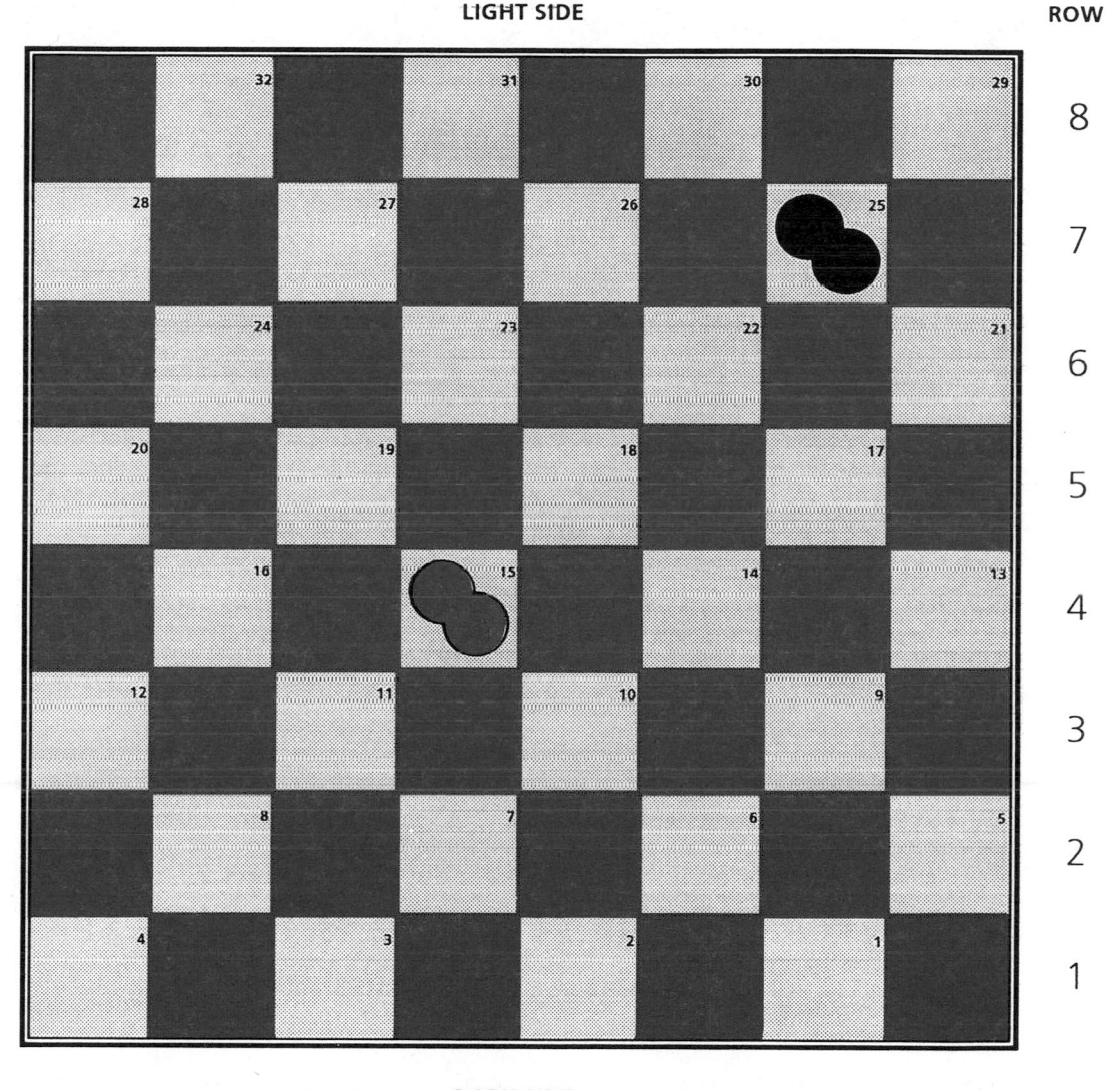

ILLUSTRATION 15: Kings can move in either direction, forward or backward, on the dark squares in any diagonal direction. The Light king on square 15 can move to four different squares and so can the Dark king on square 25. What squares can they move to? See the answers below.

Answers: The Light king on square 15 can go to squares 10, 11, 18 or 19.
The Dark king on square 25 can go to squares 21, 22, 29 or 30.

Kings are much different than single checkers which can only move or jump forward. The Kings' flexibility of movement makes them very dangerous to an opponent. (Illustrations 15 & 16)

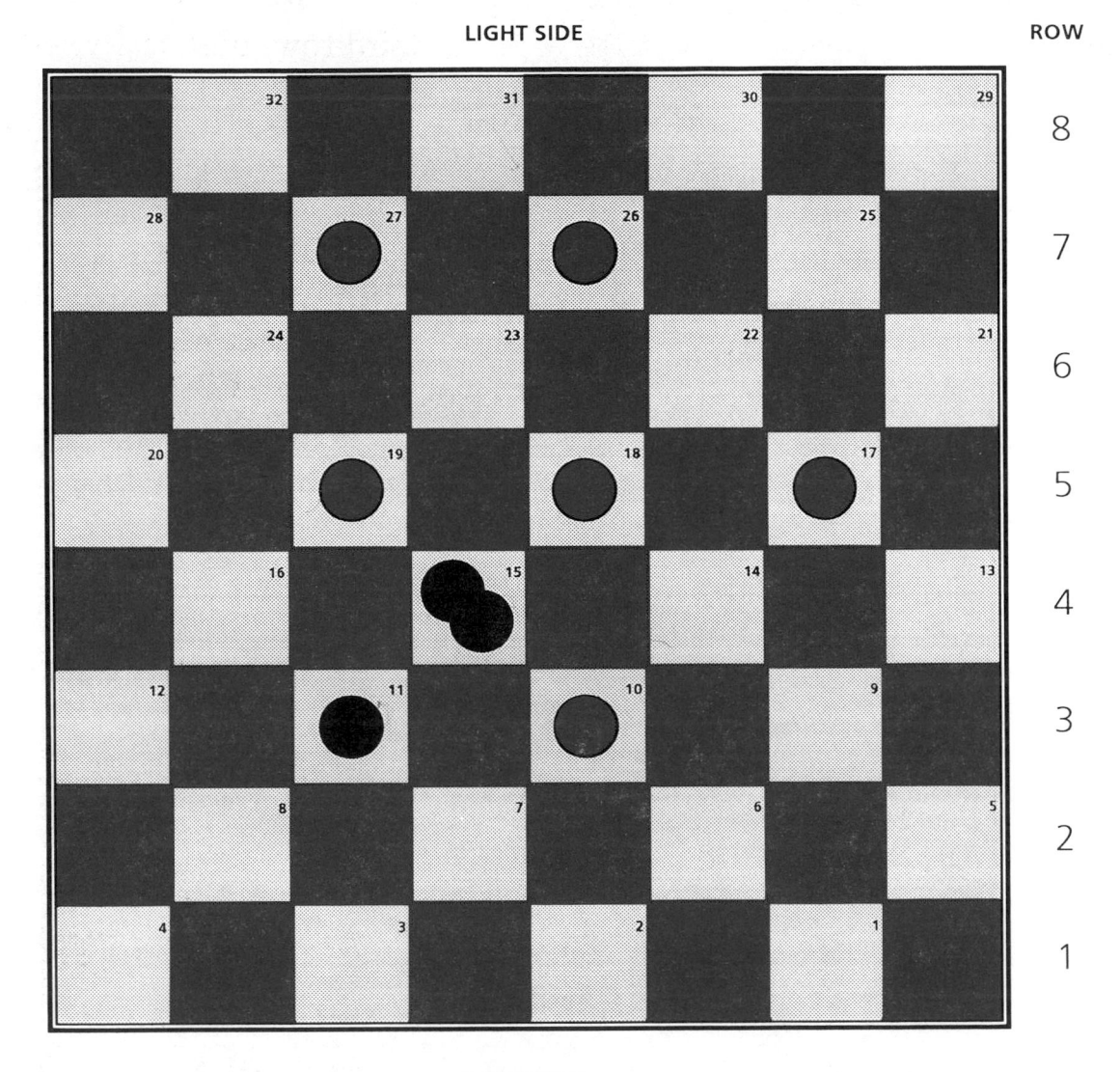

LIGHT SIDE

ROW

DARK SIDE

ILLUSTRATION 16: Kings can jump and capture the opponent's men and the opponent's kings in either direction, forward or backward, on the dark squares in any diagonal direction. Kings can keep on jumping as long as they have an opportunity. What are the most jumps that the Dark king on square 15 can make in the next turn with the pieces arranged the way you see them? #__. How would you jump? From square 15 to square __ to? to? to?

Answer: *The Dark king on square 15 can jump five Light pieces by going 15 to 22 to 31 to 24 to 15 to 6—all on the same turn: a quintuple (5) jump!*

22

STARTING AND PLAYING THE GAME

Now that you know how the checkerboard is set up and how the single checker pieces and kings move, it is time to start the game!!!

One of the Dark pieces on the squares in the third row, numbers 9, 10, 11 or 12 *always* goes first. (Illustration 17)

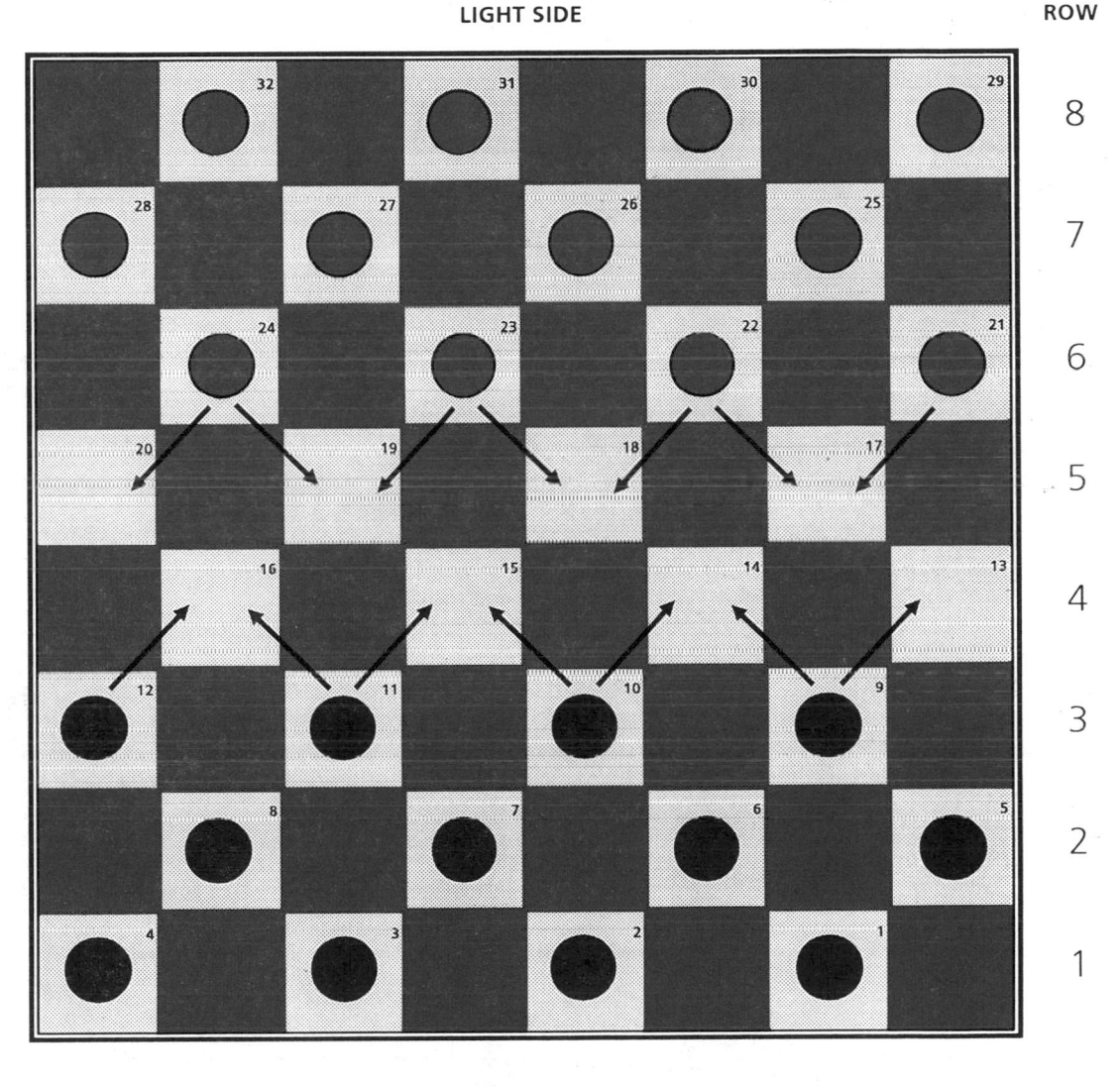

ILLUSTRATION 17: Dark has to move first and must move one of the checkers in row 3 (squares 9, 10, 11, or 12) to one of the squares in row 4 (squares 13, 14, 15, or 16) that is diagonally in front of the checker to be moved.
Next Light moves one of the checkers in the sixth row (squares 21, 22, 23, or 24) to one of the squares in the fifth row (squares 17, 18, 19, or 20) that is diagonally in front of the checker to be moved.

You and your opponent can decide who gets the Dark pieces by flipping a coin. Then, in the following games players will change colors so that they can take turns going first. Light will take the Dark checkers and Dark will take the Light checkers.

The players always take turns moving their pieces forward, Dark first, then Light, Dark again, Light again and so on until the game is won or tied.

Now that the game has started each player keeps taking turns. Dark went first, moving from square 11 to square 15. Light went next moving from square 23 to square 19. (Illustration 18)

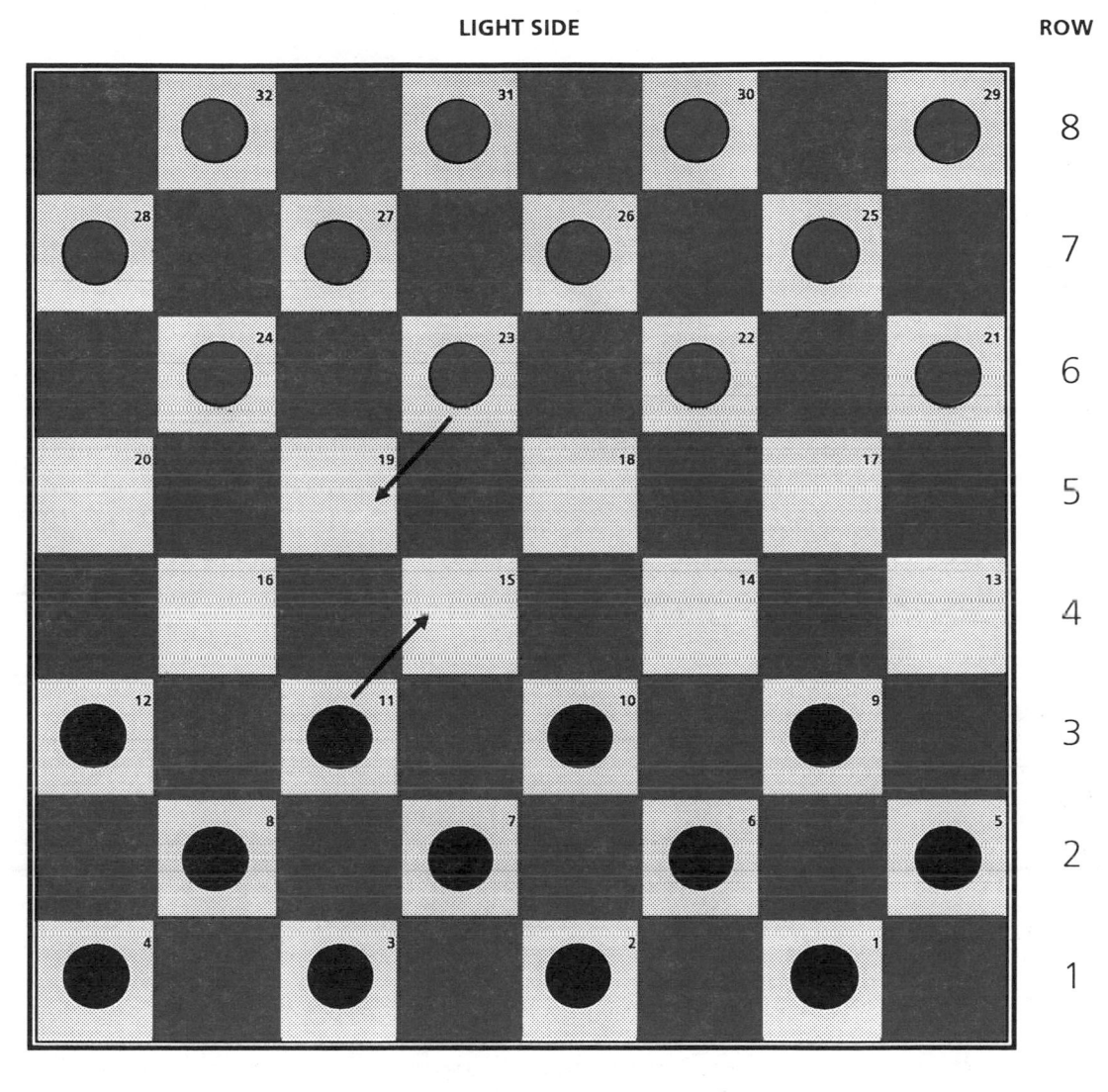

LIGHT SIDE

ROW

DARK SIDE

ILLUSTRATION 18: Dark must move first and the best move at the start is to go from square 11 diagonally forward to square 15.

Light goes next. Light's best move in this case is to go from square 23 to square 19.

25

Make these moves on your checkerboard. Whose turn is next, Dark or Light? It's Dark's turn. What move can Dark make?

Dark can go 12 to 16, 15 to 18, 8 to 11, 7 to 11, 10 to 14, 9 to 14, or 9 to 13. Dark has seven choices. Which choice is the worst?

12 to 16 is the worst because Light would jump over from 19 to 12 capturing Dark's checker on square 16 and Dark cannot jump back.

Which choice is the best? 8 to 11 because it helps to strengthen Dark's position in the center of the board. Use your checkerboard to practice these moves.

Now it is Light's turn again. What moves can Light make if Dark's second move was 8 to 11? Light can go 21 to 17, 22 to 17, 22 to 18, 26 to 23, 27 to 23, 19 to 16, or 24 to 20. Light also has seven choices.

Which of Light's choices is the worst? 19 to 16 is the worst because Dark can jump and capture the Light checker on square 16 by going 11 to 20 or 12 to 19 and Light cannot jump back.

What is Light's best move? 22 to 17 is best because it keeps Light in a safe position without giving up the center of the board.

And so the game goes on, next Dark and then Light, advancing their checkers on the Dark squares diagonally in front of them in the next row or jumping and capturing whenever possible.

Both players are trying to get to the last row on the other end of the board where their checker will be crowned king (with another checker of the same color placed on top). This makes them very, very powerful because when they are kings, they can move and jump in any diagonal direction—forward or backward.

The game continues until all of the Light or Dark checkers and kings have been captured by the other player or if the player whose turn it is, is unable to move, in which case that player loses. (Illustrations 19 & 20)

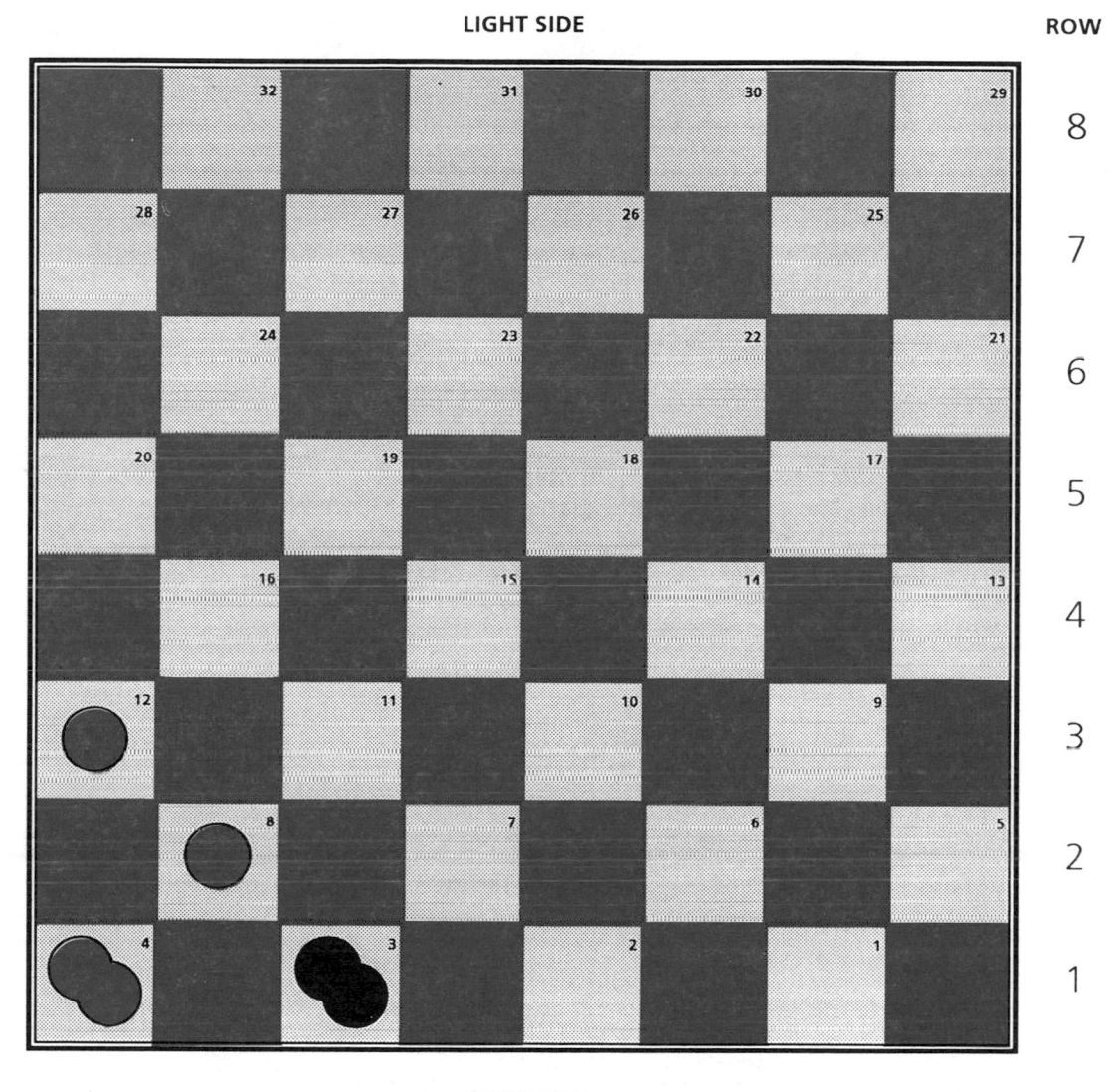

ILLUSTRATION 19: Dark wins if it is Light's move because Light cannot move! Even though Light has more pieces (two checkers and a king to Dark's one king), Dark wins because Light has nowhere to go! This is very unusual, but it does happen or you can make it happen.

Illustration 20 on the next page shows how Dark made this block happen and won.

ILLUSTRATION 20: It was Dark's turn. Dark moved the king on square 16 to square 11. Light had to jump with the Light checker on square 15 to square 8. Now Light was ahead 3 pieces to Dark's one lonely king on square 7. But when Dark moved that lonely king to square 3, it was Light's turn. And Light could not move a piece. Light lost. Dark won!

As you can see from the many choices that are available in the first two opening moves for Dark and Light there are lots of moves, jumps, double jumps, triple jumps, quadruple jumps and sacrifices (which we will show in the illustrations) that make checkers a game that you will enjoy and learn more and more about each time you play.

STRATEGY & TACTICS

Here are some ideas that will help you play a winning game.

1. Try to control the middle of the checkerboard (Illustration 21)

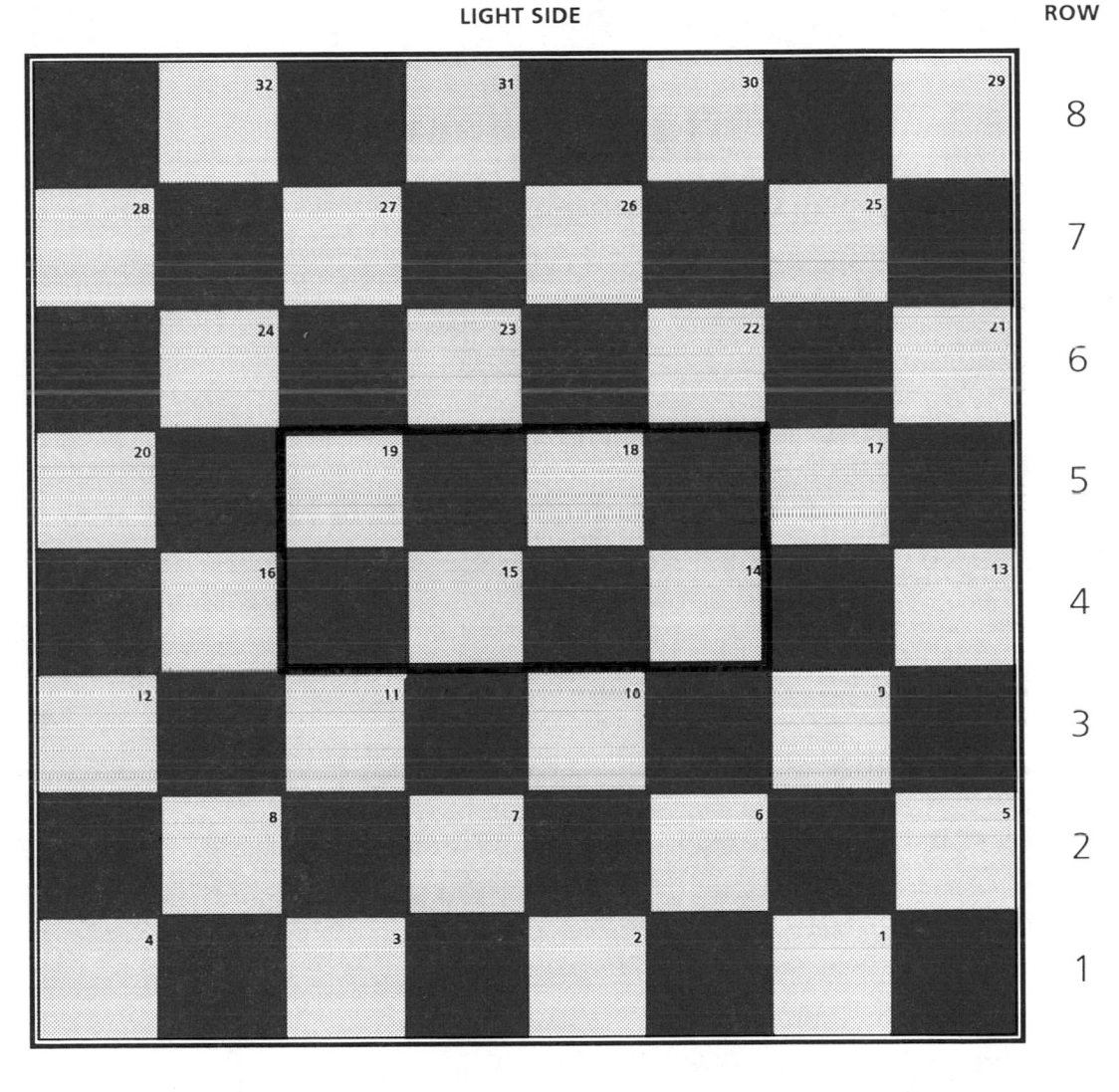

ILLUSTRATION 21: Checkers on squares 14, 15, 18, and 19 are in the center of the board. They can move and jump in a lot of different directions. This gives them more control or flexibility than a checker on square 13 or square 20 that can only move or jump in one direction.

2. Try to protect your back row (the row where your opponent gets crowned) as long as you can, (Illustration 22) by not moving your checkers out of the dark squares in your first row (1, 2, 3, & 4 for Dark and 29, 30, 31 & 32 for Light) so your opponent can't move in and get a king.

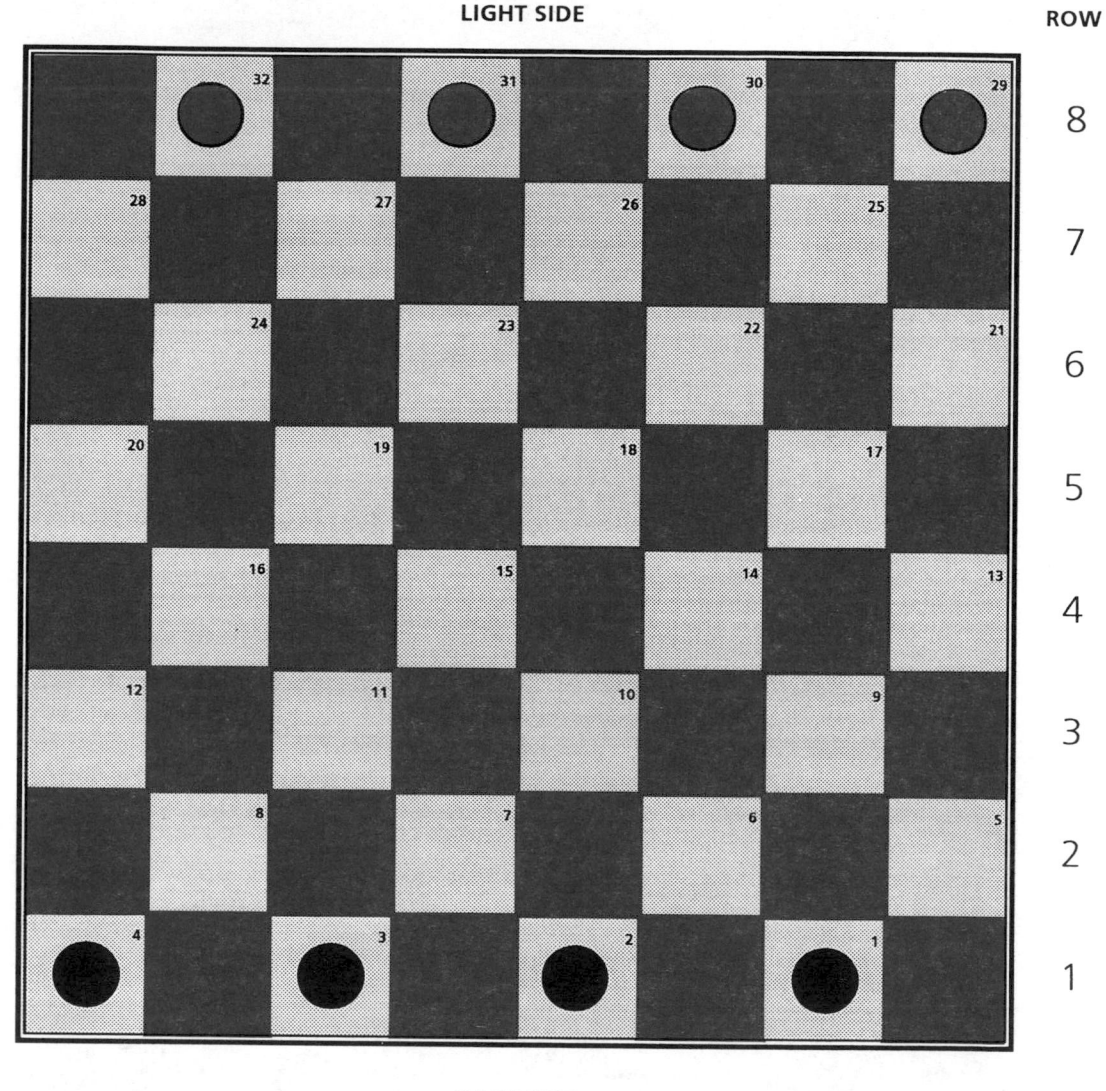

ILLUSTRATION 22: The Dark checkers in row 1 on squares 1, 2, 3, and 4 and the Light checkers in row 8 on squares 29, 30, 31, and 32 stop their opponent's checkers from getting into the king row. So, as long as you can keep these four checkers on the squares in the 1st row for Dark and the 8th row for Light, your opponent cannot get a king.

3. Look for double and triple jump opportunities (Illustration 23)

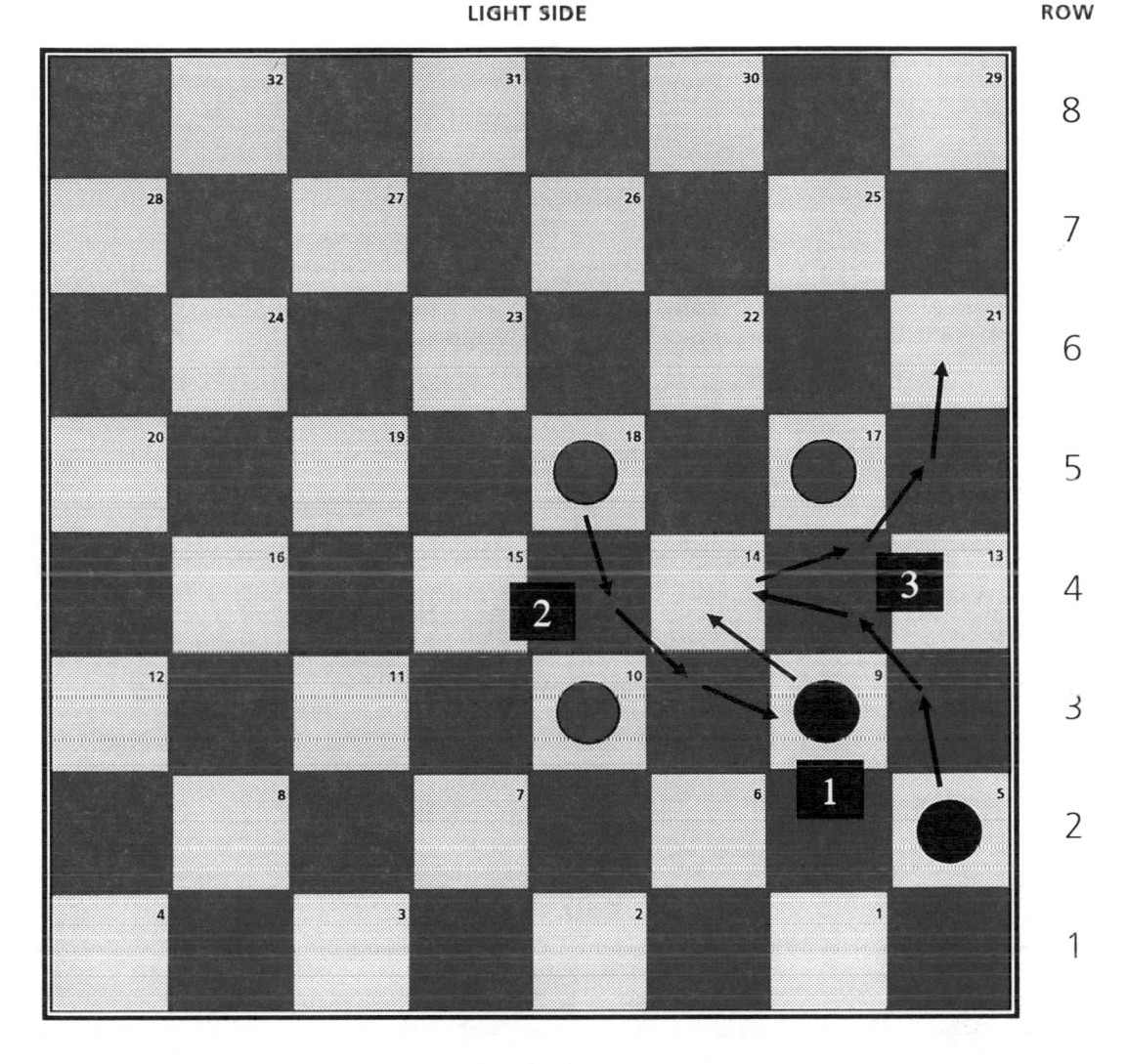

ILLUSTRATION 23: Here is a double jump opportunity! Dark moves from square 9 to square 14 sacrificing one checker because Light must jump over and capture the Dark checker on square 14 by going from square 18 to square 9. But then Dark has a double jump, going from square 5 over square 9 jumping and capturing the Light checker on square 9 and then going from square 14 to square 21 jumping over and capturing the Light checker on square 17. This is a double jump!! Dark has won two Light checkers and lost only one of the Dark checkers. A good trade for Dark!!

4. Whenever you are ahead, and you have more pieces than your opponent, it's usually (but not always) a good idea to trade piece for piece (Illustration 24)

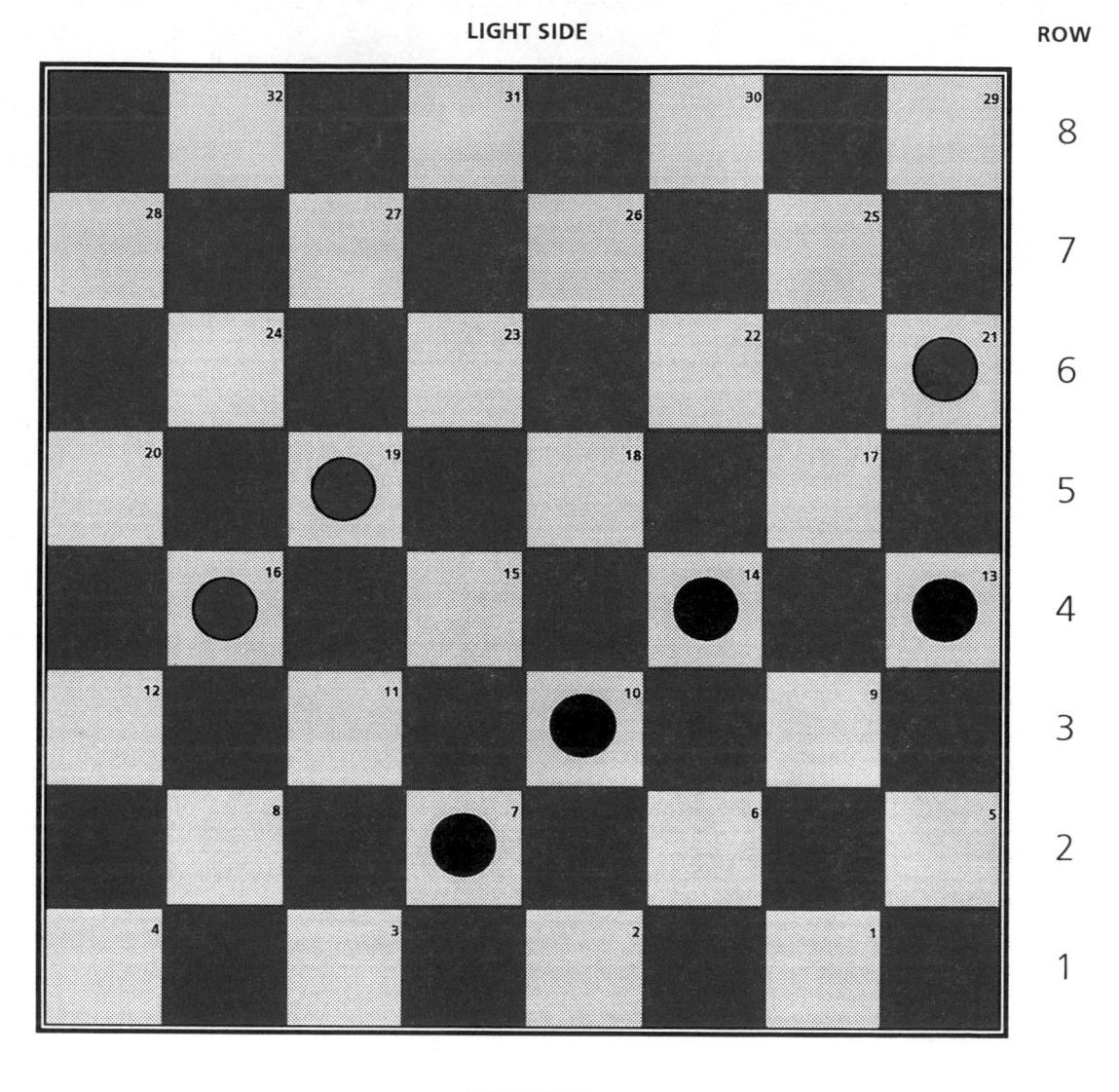

ILLUSTRATION 24: Dark's ahead with 4 checkers to Light's 3 checkers. Dark can make an even trade by moving the Dark checker on square 14 to square 17. Light must jump and capture that checker by going from square 21 to square 14. But then Dark can jump right back with the checker on square 10 going over the Light checker on square 14 to square 17. An even trade and Dark's still ahead 3 to 2!

5.   When you have to move pieces from your back row (row 1 for Dark and row 8 for Light) move the far left end checker first (square #4 for Dark and square #29 for Light). Next move the third from the left (square #2 for Dark and square #31 for Light). This still makes it hard for your opponent to get his checkers into his king row. (Illustration 25)

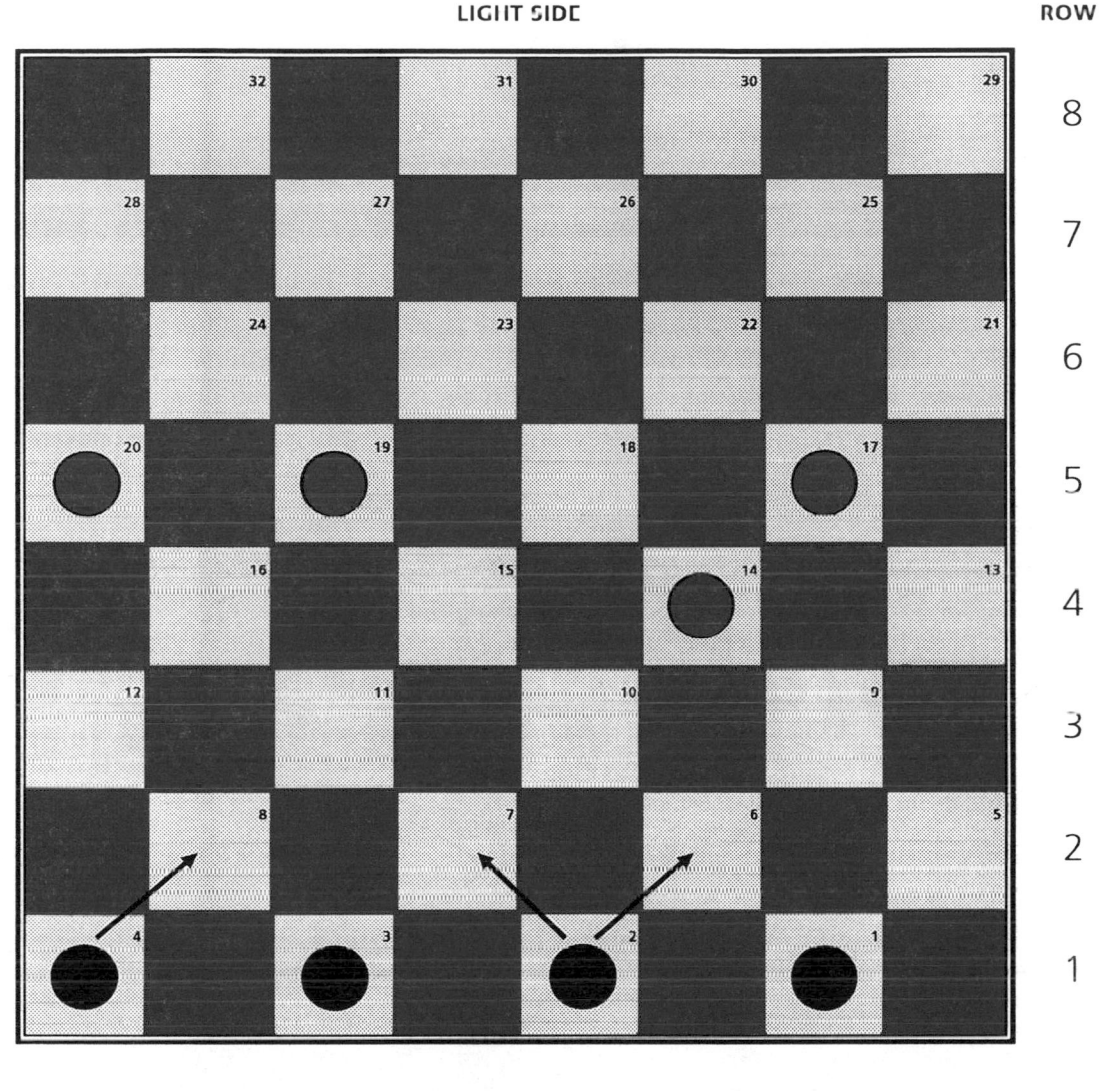

ILLUSTRATION 25: Dark's turn to move. Dark has to move one of the checkers out of Light's king row (row 1). It's usually best to move out from the single corner first (square 4 for Dark and square 29 for Light) because that's the most difficult for the opponent to get into if there is a checker on square 3, because you can only go in one way (from 11 to 8 to 4) if square 12 is occupied. And you can't get in at all if square 12 isn't occupied. Next it's best to move out from square 2 (Dark) or square 31 (Light) because this still makes it difficult for the opponent to move into the king row and the opponent must put a checker piece on square 10 for Light and square 23 for Dark so that another piece can move into the king row without being jumped. The worst piece to move out early is the checker in the double corner (square #1 for Dark and square #32 for Light) because that makes it very easy for the opponent to get into the king row.

35

6. When it is your move, look for ways to trade or sacrifice one of your pieces or kings for two of your opponent's pieces or kings. By giving up (sacrificing) one of your pieces or kings to force your opponent to jump and capture it, you may expose his pieces to a double or triple jump by your checker or king (Illustrations 26 and 27). Set up your checkerboard and practice these moves.

LIGHT SIDE   **ROW**

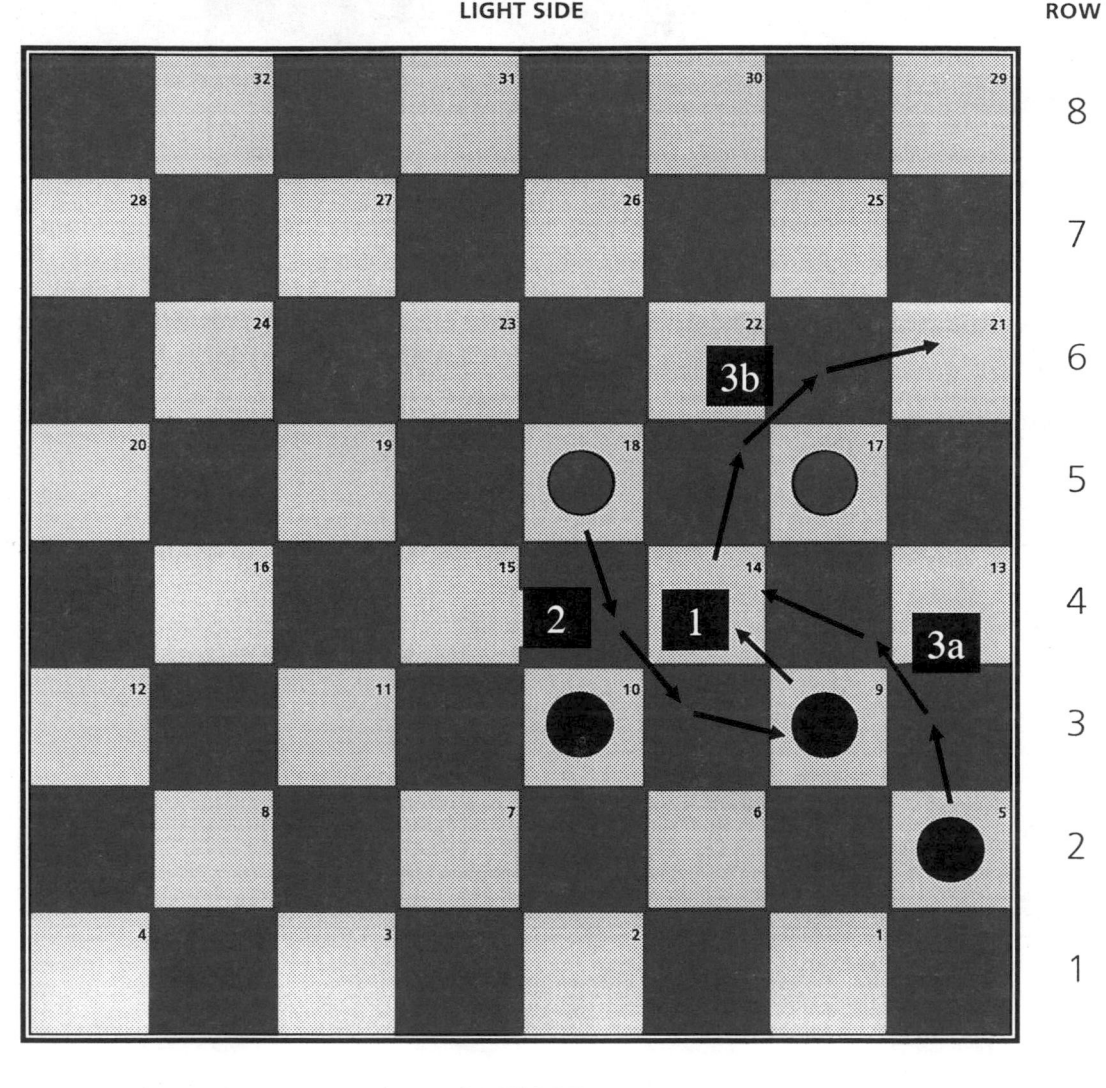

DARK SIDE

ILLUSTRATION 26: Dark's move. Dark can get a double jump by sacrificing the Dark checker on square 9. To do this, Dark moves the checker on square 9 to square 14. Light has to jump and capture this checker with the Light checker on square 18 going to square 9. But then Dark has a double jump going from square 5 over Light's checker on square 9 to square 14 and then jumping again over Light's checker on square 17 to square 21. All of Light's checkers have been captured—Dark wins!!

36

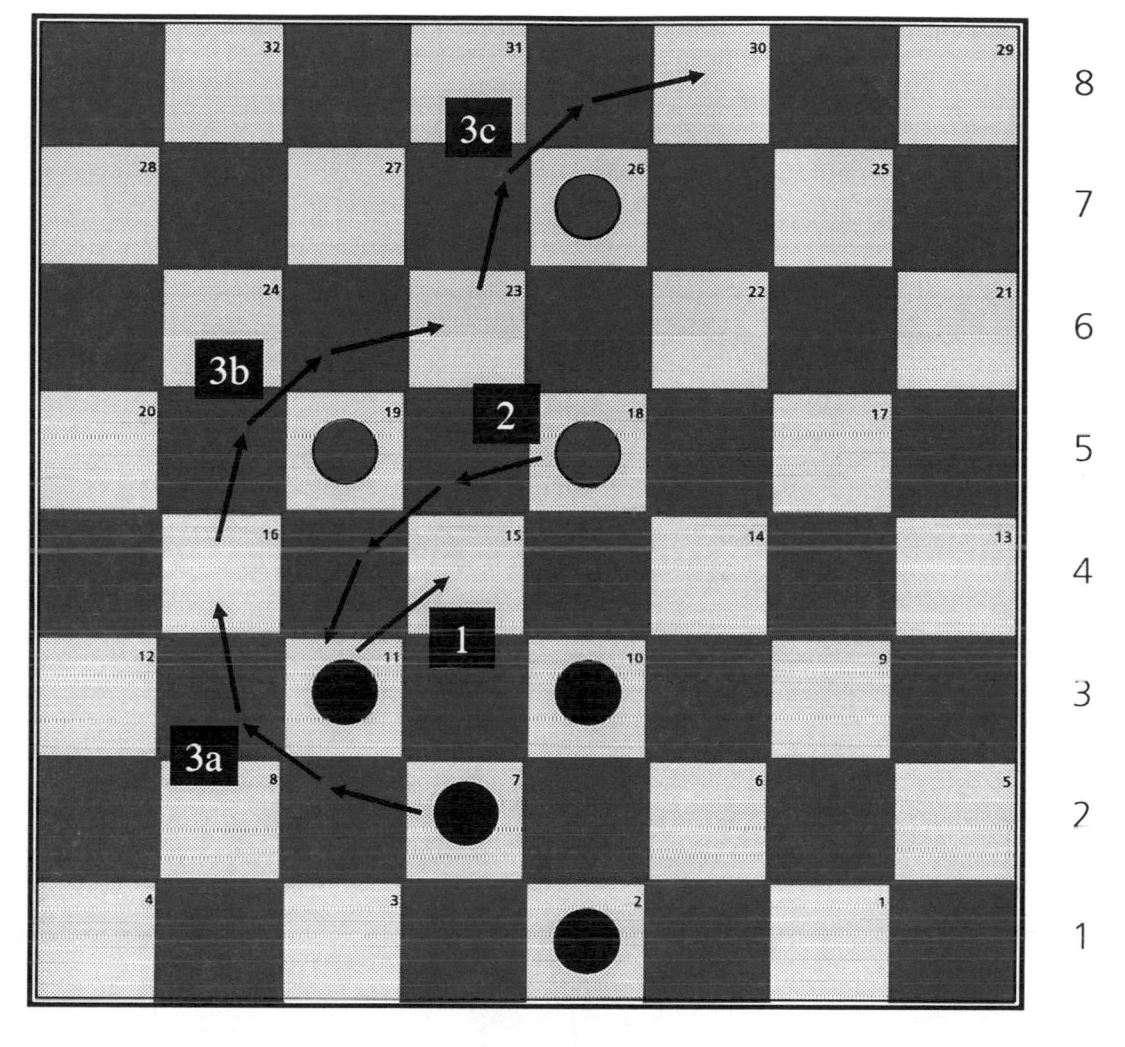

ILLUSTRATION 27: Dark's turn. Dark can get a triple jump by sacrificing the Dark checker on square 11. To do this, Dark moves the checker on square 11 to square 15. Light has to jump and capture this piece with the checker on square 18 going over to square 11. But then Dark gets a triple jump—going from square 7 to square 16 from 16 to 23 and from 23 to 30; capturing all three of Light's pieces in one move! Light doesn't have any more pieces left—Dark wins!

7. Before you make a move, think about what your opponent might be able to do when it is his turn. Think about defending your position as well as what offensive moves you might make—remember it's better to draw or tie than to lose and a lot of checker games end in a draw.

WINNING THE GAME

As the game goes on, single checker pieces and kings are jumped and captured by each side until only a few Dark and Light pieces are still left on the board.

Remember, the winner is the player who has a checker or a king still left on the board when the opponent does not have any checkers or kings left. That player wins!!

So, if you have more checkers and kings than your opponent does toward the end of the game, you can trade or sacrifice one of your pieces for one of your opponent's pieces by sacrifice jumps. (Refer to Illustration 22) As soon as you can capture all of your opponent's pieces by jumping over them, you will win. (Illustration 2)

If your opponent captures all of your pieces by jumping over them, your opponent wins and you lose. If both you and your opponent have an equal number of pieces toward the end of the game (usually kings or potential kings) and are equally positioned on the checkerboard, you probably have a draw or a tie, and no one wins. (Refer to Illustration 1)

Look at the following checkerboard illustrations to see if you can tell who is going to win or draw.   (Illustration 28)

(Illustration 29)

(Illustration 30)

LIGHT SIDE   **ROW**

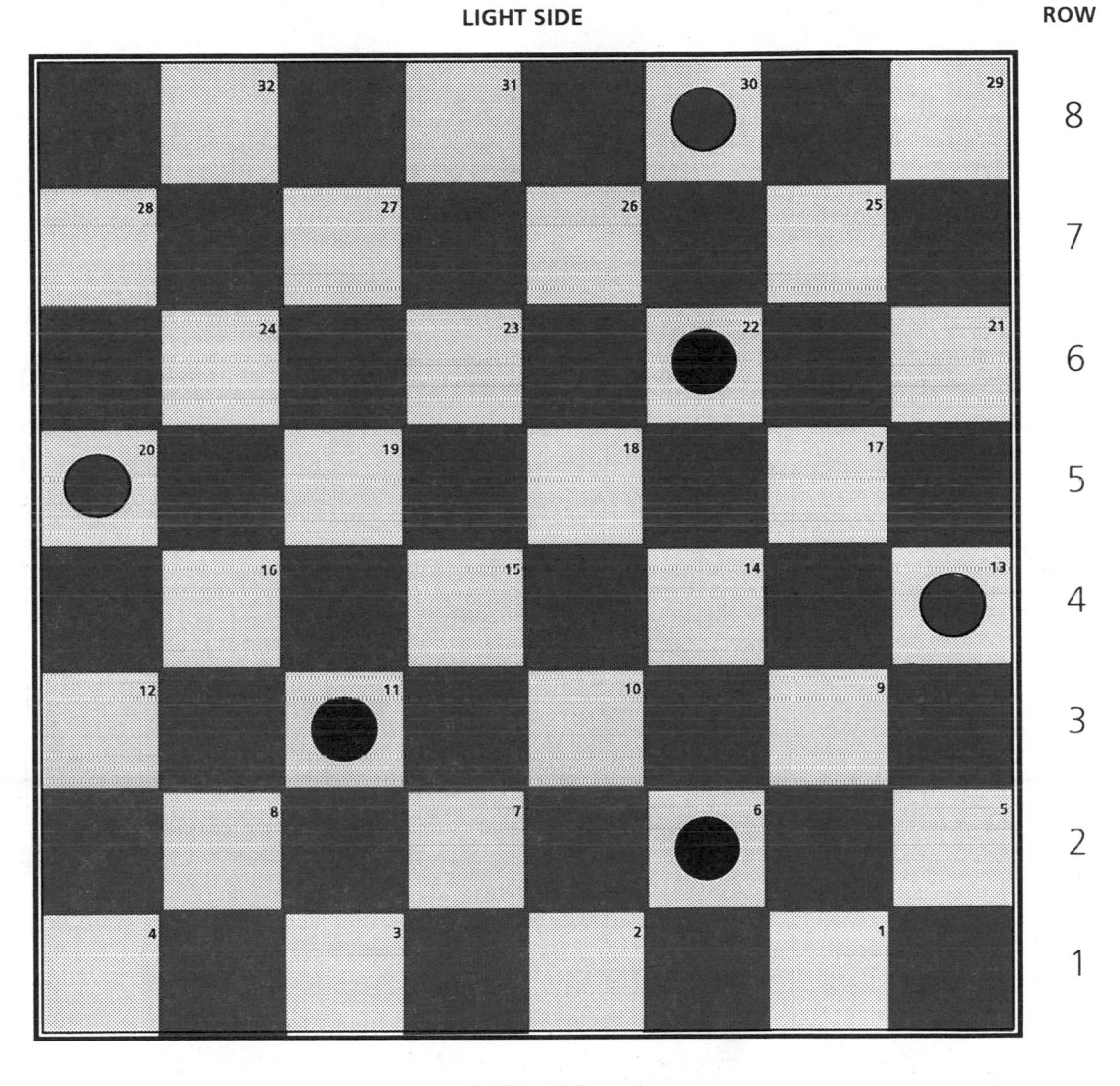

DARK SIDE

ILLUSTRATION 28: It's Light's turn to move. Who wins? Dark wins! Why does Dark win? Because whatever move Light makes (20 to 16, 13 to 9, or 30 to 26, or 30 to 25) Dark will get a jump and capture. So in three moves Light will lose all of the three Light checkers and the game!

LIGHT SIDE

ROW

8
7
6
5
4
3
2
1

DARK SIDE

ILLUSTRATION 29: It's Dark's turn to move. Who wins? This time Light wins! Why? Because whatever move Dark makes, Light will get to jump and capture the Dark checker that moved. So in three moves, Light will capture all of Dark's checkers. Try this setup on your board. It shows how important having to move can be. For example, if it was Light's turn to move in this same situation what would happen? Dark would win instead of Light because Light would have to move into a jump no matter where Light moved!

42

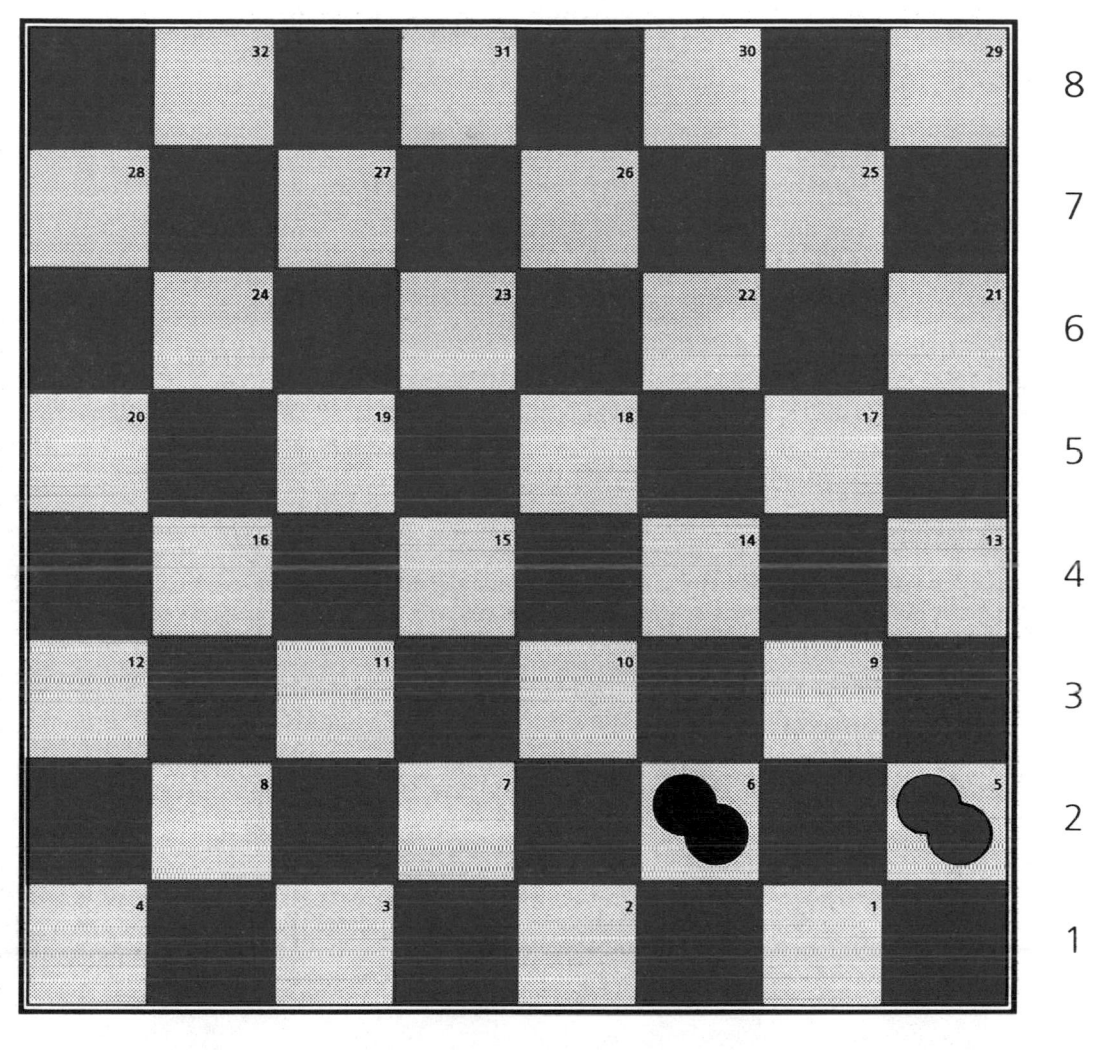

ILLUSTRATION 30: Who will win this game? Dark? or Light? No one will win. Why not? Because both Light and Dark have one king and neither can force the other into a position where they can get a jump unless the opponent makes a very bad move. So it's a tie game or a draw—no one wins—no one loses. And in this case it doesn't matter who moves first.

43

Toward the end of the game, if one player has a lot more kings and/or checkers than the other player, its ok for the player who is obviously way behind and is going to lose to surrender. (Illustration 31) *But* be careful before you surrender, because sometimes you can find a special move or series of moves that will get you back in the game so you can tie or even win. *Never give up easily!*

ILLUSTRATION 31: Dark has four kings and two checker pieces. Light only has one king and two checker pieces. And Light's pieces are all separated so they can't help each other. Almost as soon as they move they are going to be attacked and jumped by Dark's pieces. So while Light can make a few more moves, there isn't any real hope of winning or even getting a tie game. Once Light realizes this, he surrenders and says to Dark, "You win." Then they can start another game instead of wasting time.

Here are three more illustrated checkerboard situations (Illustrations 32, 33 & 34) for you to study and figure out what moves to make. Try them out.

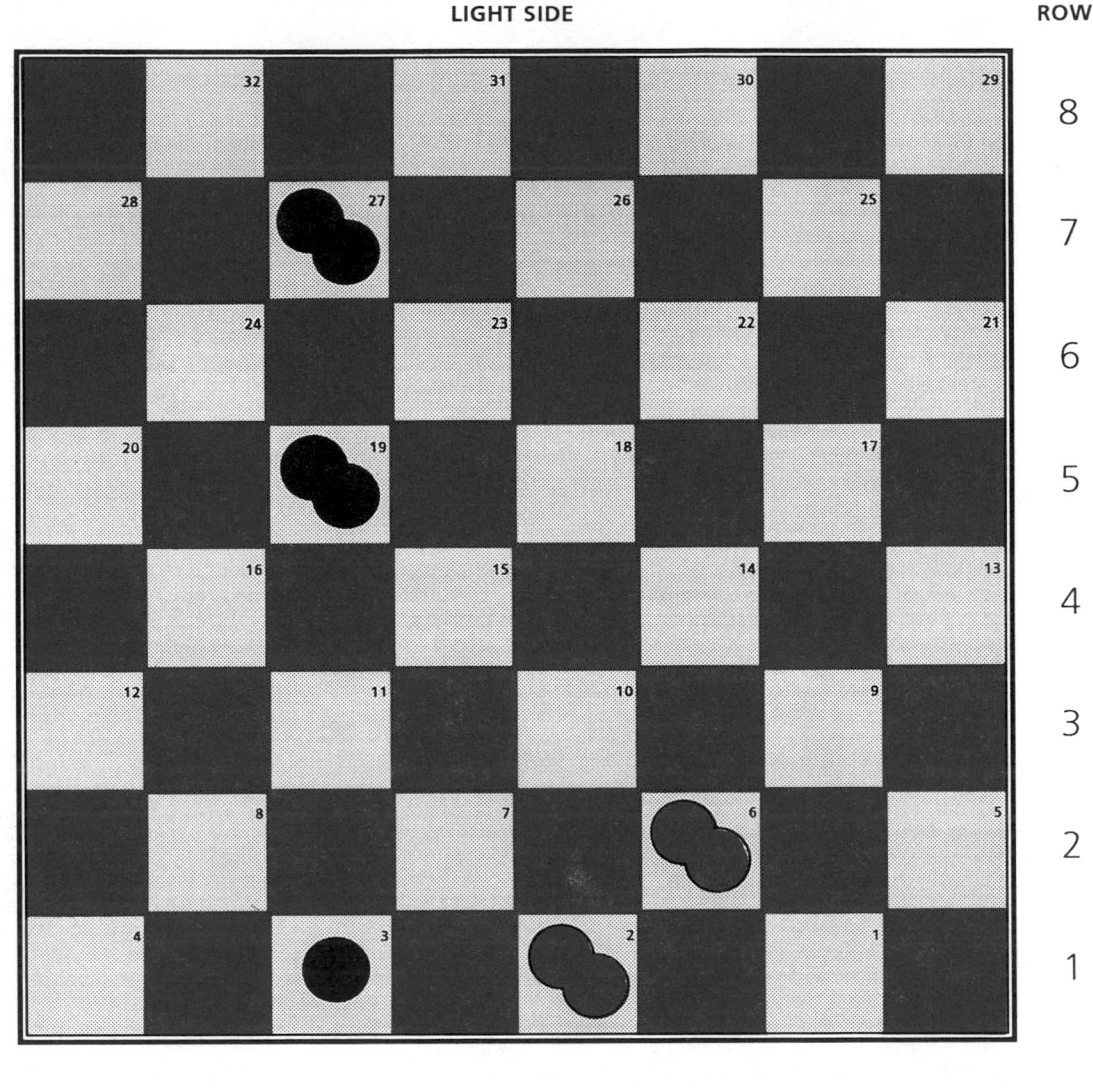

ILLUSTRATION 32: *It's Light's turn to move. Can Light win even though he only has two pieces while Dark has three? Yes, Light can win if he makes the right move. What is the right move? Do you see it? Answer: Light wins by going from square 2 to square 7 and sacrificing his king. What a move!! Dark has to jump Light's king on square 7 with his single checker on square 3 going from square 3 to square 10. But then Light's king on square 6 has a triple jump going from square 6 to square 15 to square 24 to square 31. Light captures all of Dark's remaining pieces with this awesome move and wins the game!!*

ROW

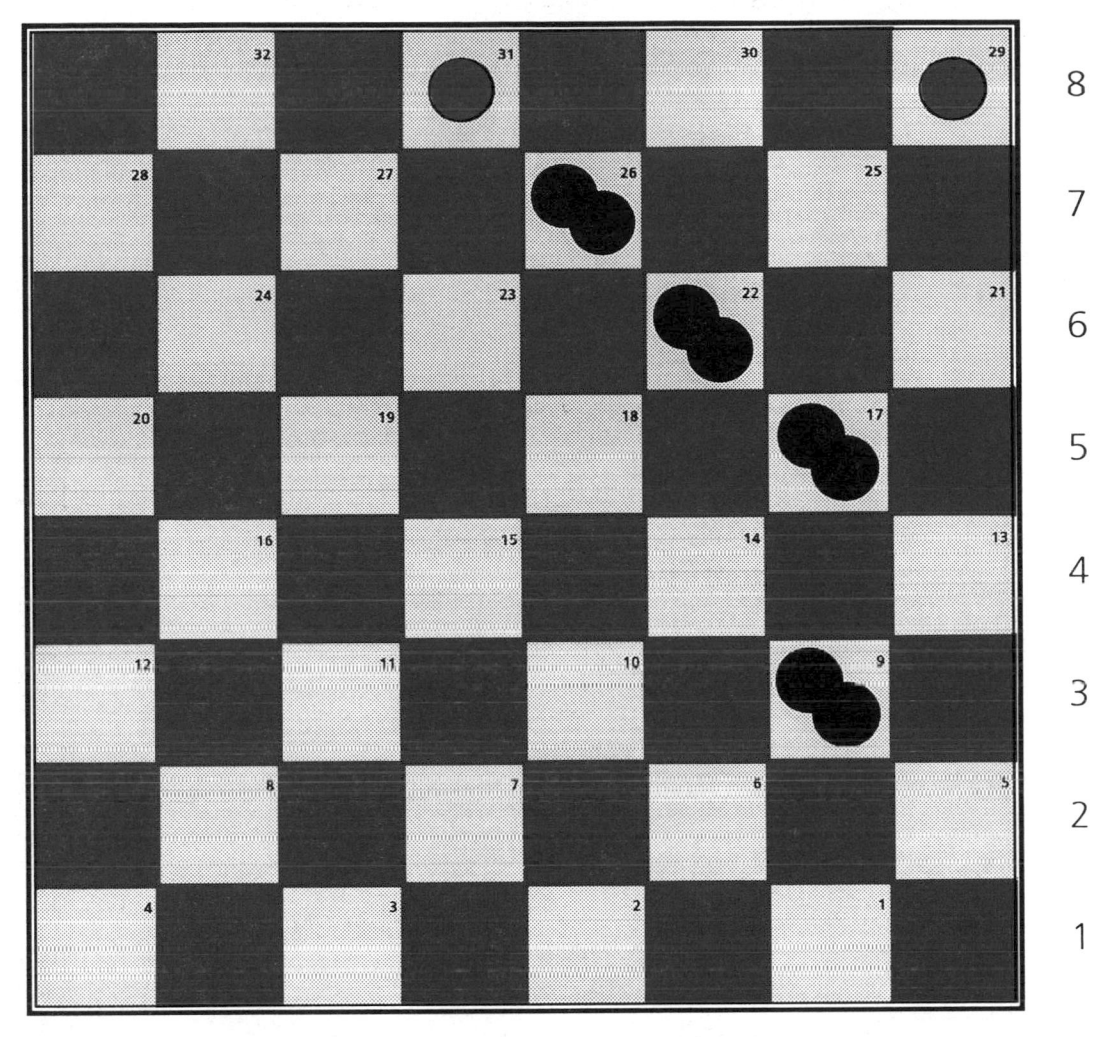

				8
				7
				6
				5
				4
				3
				2
				1

DARK SIDE

ILLUSTRATION 33: It's Light's turn to move. It looks like Dark is going to win. Light only has two single checker pieces and Dark has four kings. But Light can get a tie if he makes the right move. Can you find the right move for Light? What is it?

Answer: *Light should go from square 29 to square 25 sacrificing that checker. The Dark king on square 22 has to jump Light's checker on square 25 going to square 29. But now Light has a triple jump! His last man on square 31 jumps to square 22 then to square 13 and finally to square 6.*

Now each player has one piece left. Dark's king can come out of the single corner, but Light gets a king on the next move. Now they are even. Each player has one king. Neither player can trap the other into a jump. It's a tie!

And this is why you never surrender or give up until you've explored all the different possibilities.

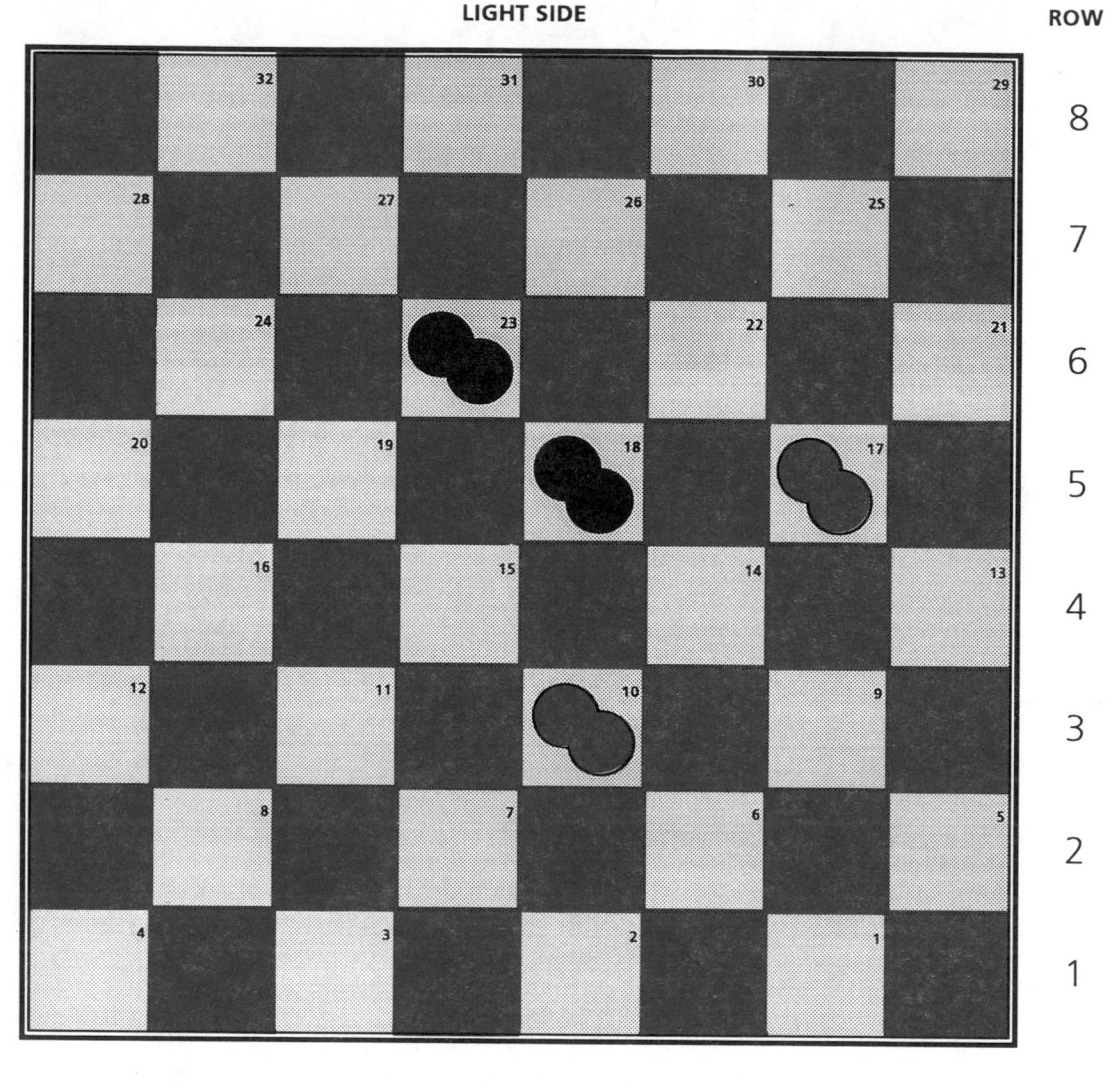

DARK SIDE

ILLUSTRATION 34: It's Dark's turn. Both players have two kings. Is it an even game? Will it end in a tie? No! Can Dark win? Yes! How can Dark win? Dark can win by going from square 18 to square 14 with his king. Good move! Now, if Light moves the king on square 17, Dark's king on 18 will jump the Light king on square 10. If Light moves his king on square 10, Dark will jump the Light king on square 17. Then Dark will have two kings to Light's one king. And Dark can force a win.

Try to avoid the position that Light got into with an empty dark square in between two of your men.

Also this situation teaches us not to declare a tie until we make sure there is no way to win.

The end of this book is just the beginning of your becoming a checker player—a good, or an excellent, or even a champion checker player.

It is a beginning or a start, because the best way to learn is to play and practice against opponents, against yourself or against a computer. You can also learn a lot by reading other checker books. From these you will learn the moves the champion players make to win. There is an old and very true saying, "Experience is the best teacher" and another that says "practice makes perfect."

If you play and practice checkers with your friends and family you will keep on learning more about the game and the rules. You will learn to make good moves and to avoid bad moves. You will find out about the winning strategies and what moves aren't so good.

And you will become a better and better checker player. Most importantly, you will appreciate the beauty of this wonderful game with all of its fantastic combinations of moves and enjoy it forever! This book cannot end by wishing you good luck, because on page 2 we told you there is no luck in checkers—only skill, but we do wish you a lifetime of fun with checkers.

BASIC RULES OF CHECKERS

1. The Checkerboard

The Checkerboard must be square in shape and made up of 32 light squares and 32 dark squares. The board is placed between the two players so that each has a dark single corner at the far left side. The dark squares are numbered 1-32 and the light squares do not have numbers.

2. The Checkers (also called single checker pieces or men)

There are 24 checkers used to play the game. They are divided equally, 12 Light and 12 Dark. The checkers should be disc shaped, round and flat.

3. Starting position and movement of the checkers

The checkers are placed and move only on the dark squares. To start, the Dark checkers are placed on the first twelve dark squares, numbered 1-12. The Light checkers go on the last 12 dark squares numbered 21-32. Light and Dark checkers can only move or jump forward diagonally to an empty dark square in the row(s) ahead.

4. Order of Play

Dark always goes first. Players choose colors by flipping a coin. After each game they switch sides and colors.

5. Jumping and capturing moves

If a jump is available, it *must* be taken. If two or more jumping opportunities are available, the player who must make the jumping move has the choice of which jump to take. When jumping into the king row with a single checkerpiece, the move ends there. The single checker piece is crowned a king. It cannot move again until the opponent has taken a turn, even if there is another jumping move available.

6. Crowning kings and their movement

When a single checker piece reaches any of the squares in the last row on the far end of the board it must be crowned a king by placing another checker of the same color on top of the single checker.

Kings can move and jump diagonally in any direction on the dark squares—forward or backward.

7. Tied or drawn games

A game is tied (drawn) when neither side can force the other into jumping situations that would result in captures or into blocked positions where the opponent could not make a move when it was his turn.

8. Winning games

A player wins when he captures all of his opponent's pieces (kings and single checkers) or blocks all of his opponent's pieces so they cannot move when it is their turn to go.

LIGHT SIDE

DARK SIDE

If you do not have a numbered checkerboard, cut this one out along the dotted lines, paste it to an equally sized piece of cardboard and use pennies (dark) and dimes (light) for your checker pieces.

53